COGNITIVE-BEHAVIOR THERAPY

CURRENT ISSUES IN BEHAVIORAL PSYCHOLOGY

Series Editor

Robert S. Ruskin, Ph.D.
Chairman, Department of Psychology and
Director, Center for Personalized Instruction
Georgetown University
Washington, D.C.

Other Books in this Series

The Social Skills Basis of Psychopathology
E. Lakin Phillips, Ph.D.

Therapy and Ethics:
The Courtship of Law and Psychology
Norman J. Finkel, Ph.D.

Educating Disturbed Adolescents:
Theory and Practice
Peyton Towns

COGNITIVE-BEHAVIOR THERAPY

A Restructuring Approach

Rian E. McMullin, Ph.D.
Director, Counseling Research Institute
Lakewood, Colorado

Thomas R. Giles, M.S.
School of Professional Psychology
University of Denver
Denver, Colorado
Behavior Therapy Unit
School of Medicine
Temple University
Philadelphia, Pennsylvania

GRUNE & STRATTON
A Subsidiary of Harcourt Brace Jovanovich, Publishers
New York London Toronto Sydney San Francisco

Library of Congress Cataloging in Publication Data

McMullin, Rian E.
Cognitive-behavior therapy.

(Current issues in behavioral psychology)
Includes bibliographical references and index.
1. Cognitive therapy. 2. Behavior therapy.
I. Giles, Thomas R. II. Title. III. Series. [DNLM:
1. Behavior therapy—Methods. 2. Cognition. WM 425
M478c]
RC489.C63M35 616.89′142 81-4960
ISBN 0-8089-1362-X AACR2

Grune & Stratton, Inc.
111 Fifth Avenue
New York, New York 10003

Distributed in the United Kingdom by
Academic Press Inc. (London) Ltd.
24/28 Oval Road, London NW 1

Library of Congress Catalog Number 81-4960
International Standard Book Number 0-8089-1362-X

Printed in the United States of America

The authors dedicate this book to their parents.

The first author dedicates the book to his mother, Mary R. McMullin.

The second author dedicates his work on this volume to his parents, Jack and Marian Giles, whose love and support made many good things possible.

Contents

Part IV Therapeutic Interventions

Acknowledgments

The authors wish to thank William Casey who helped develop some of the cognitive restructuring techniques. They also wish to thank Drs. Frederick Todd and Evelyn Paley who made valuable critical comments and suggestions while reviewing the original manuscript. The authors further acknowledge the contributions of Dorene Millick, Jackie Briggs, Christine Eitemiller, JoAnna Deu Pree, Linda and Michele, Andrew Sweet, and Geri Wolfson. The second author is especially grateful for the support, guidance, and friendship of Drs. Todd and Paley.

Foreword

It is a pleasure to welcome *Cognitive-Behavior Therapy: A Restructuring Approach* to our series. The careful integration of cognitive techniques into the framework of existing behavioral therapies has proven to be one of the more important recent advances in clinical practice. Many therapists routinely employ cognitive techniques yet fail to appreciate the theoretical underpinnings of their usage. The present book is well-designed by authors McMullin and Giles to provide the practicing clinician with a clear, concise description of both cognitive and behavioral techniques and, perhaps more importantly, to provide precise step-by-step implementation procedures necessary for successful use of these techniques. I suspect that you will find the book as enlightening as I did.

Robert S. Ruskin, Ph.D.

1
Introduction

Since the early 1960s, clinical psychologists have become increasingly interested in the use of cognitive theory and methodology in psychotherapy (Meichenbaum, 1977). Given the relatively new status of the mushrooming field of cognitive therapy, it is understandable that there are gaps in present knowledge. On the one hand, from a clinical point of view, the seminal contributions of Albert Ellis (see, e.g., 1962; 1974; 1975) have served as the preeminent guide to cognitive therapy. But Ellis's theoretical conceptions—which are derived largely from the Stoic philosophies (Ellis, 1974)—sometimes lend themselves more to the epistemology of eloquent rhetoric than to the rigors of scientific methodology. Perhaps as a result, Rational Emotive Therapy (RET) lacks the systematic procedural guidelines that characterize other behaviorist and neobehaviorist techniques (e.g., Azrin & Nunn, 1978; Jacobson & Margolin, 1979; Sutherland, Amit, & Weiner, 1977).

On the other hand, many excellent recent volumes have developed from empirical philosophy and review the latest applications of learning theory and cognitive research (e.g., Foreyt & Rathjen, 1978; Kendall & Hollon, 1979; Mahoney, 1974; Meichenbaum, 1977). Although the clinical procedures discussed in these books are more systematically delineated and applied than are their rational-emotive counterparts, several shortcomings continue to exist. First and foremost, these contributions tend to support the contention that cognitive-behavior therapy is the simple and unvaried application of technique to problem. Thus, a phobia is treated with some variant of systematic desensitization, an obsession with thought-stopping, free-floating anxiety with RET, "impulsivity" with cognitive rehearsal, and so on.

We would emphasize that no therapeutic technique, cognitive or otherwise, is applicable to every occurrence of a clinical problem. Todd (1980) has reported successfully treating four cases of obsessive-compulsive disorders using a different set of therapeutic interventions in each instance. In one of these cases, the major intervention was operant marital counseling. Thus, a particular technique is properly applied *after* a functional assessment has been made. We discuss the procedure for making such an assessment in Chapter 3.

Another drawback of the literature that focuses largely on research and on reviews of research is that it pays little attention to the complexities and variations in human problems that surface in therapists' consulting rooms. A significant treatment effect, although extremely important in its own right, does not adequately address the many questions therapists often face. For example,

- What degree of relationship building is needed to encourage compliance with therapeutic directives?
- How often does resistance to interventions occur, and what measures are available to handle such resistance?
- What verbatim means of persuasion are used to prepare subjects for therapeutic conceptions, homework assignments, etc.?
- What measures best predict success or failure as treatment progresses?
- What techniques are necessary to enhance maintenance gains?
- How exactly does the therapist implement therapeutic techniques in clinical practice?
- What complications or special problems arise during treatment, and what adaptations of the therapy are available to handle these problems?
- How does the clinician know when to apply one technique rather than another?

In general the literature does not provide enough detail for therapists to apply cognitive techniques properly.

The present volume addresses the above and other questions within a clinical methodology derived from experience, current theory, and research. Assessment is stressed throughout, so that the reader will know when (and when not) to apply the appropriate cognitive techniques. Finally, the *cognitive restructuring therapy* (CRT) herein described has been systematically defined in order to improve treatment efficacy and efficiency. An average of 15 sessions per client is common with this approach.

Two general comments on the present volume's structure and style of presentation are in order. First, the theoretical section presented in Chapter 1 discusses the current empirical perspectives from which our cognitive restructuring techniques were derived. We have included this section in order to emphasize the coordination of theory with technique and to delineate the assumptions on which the therapy is based. The reader will find this section highly technical, however, and more difficult to read and understand than the rest of the book.

Second, the style in which this book is written has been greatly influenced by the combination of events that produced the work. Greatly interested in learning theory, behavior therapy and assessment, and paradoxical techniques, author Giles was attracted to the CRT approach as author McMullin had developed it over a period of 10 years. As a result, McMullin trained Giles in the use of CRT. This book grew out of the authors' taped conversations of supervision sessions, and both authors collaborated equally in the development of the manuscript. Thus the material here is presented from the point of view of one who is trying to learn the restructuring therapy. We have included verbatim examples, stepwise procedural guidelines, rationales for the techniques, and other concepts primarily designed to be clear, concise, and informative. The reader who attempts to absorb this work in one sitting is thus guaranteed an exercise in concentration (and probably a headache). We recommend that one read only a few chapters at a time and review and reread the chapters before applying the techniques described.

PART I

Theoretical Perspectives

This section clarifies the authors' bias towards empirical explanations of behavior. We review recent advances in learning theory and present a rationale for using cognitive techniques. Additional theoretical explanations for the development and efficacy of our therapy can be found in Parts III and IV.

2

Cognitive-Behavior Therapy: Historical and Current Perspectives

It is our belief that psychological theory is an extremely important if not essential ingredient in the practice of effective psychotherapy. As Yates (1975) has argued, theory should explicitly guide therapeutic technique by helping us to select from a conglomerate of client behaviors, the true dependent variables and their functional contributors in need of change (see Chapter 4). A theory helps the clinician decide whether a dream about snakes is psychologically significant or "just so much noise."

As also pointed out by Yates, in contrast to the views of Arthur (1971, 1972), Lazarus (1971), and London (1972), innovations in applied technology often develop from an underlying theoretical base and are later evaluated on the basis of such a theory. The conception of phobias as learned maladaptive autonomic habits (Wolpe, 1958), for instance, has led to several highly effective treatment techniques designed to condition anxiety-competitive responses to phobia-inducing stimuli (e.g., Wolpe, 1958, 1973).

It is also our view that cognitive-behavior therapy developed from, and is in large measure encompassed by, behavior therapy itself and thus, like behavior therapy, claims an empirical base. We are in agreement, then, with Wilson's (1978) contention that cognitive-behavior therapy can be best understood by means of the theoretical underpinnings from which it evolved.

Given our affinity for theory in general and learning theory in particular, we are faced with a problem of some complexity. In the 1960s and

1970s, several time-honored assumptions of learning theory were largely disconfirmed (Bolles, 1975), and this upheaval has generated radical changes in the explanation of learning phenomena. As Bandura (1965, 1969), Bolles (1975), Breger and McGaugh (1965), Mahoney (1974), Meichenbaum (1977), Millenson and Leslie (1979), Schwartz (1978), Seligman (1970, 1971), and others have argued, the laws of learning are much more complicated than was once believed. These authors' contributions have extended behavior theory to include thoughts, feelings, genetic and biological "blueprints," and other variables in the causal realm of behavioral events. Since cognitive behavior therapy has developed largely from elaborations of these researchers, the section that follows will describe briefly how this synthesis of ideas has evolved. The reader who is unfamiliar with the very considerable literature on the material to be discussed may wish to consult the references cited throughout the next section.

THREE FUNDAMENTAL ASSUMPTIONS OF LEARNING THEORY DISCONFIRMED

The Correspondence Assumption

Traditional learning theorists (e.g., Thorndike, 1911; Watson, 1914; Guthrie, 1935) believed that all learning is accompanied by a corresponding augmentation of underlying (psychological) stimulus–response (S–R) bonds. Many theorists also believed that a corresponding neural strengthening was involved (Bolles, 1975). The stimulus–response bond was thus assumed to be isomorphic with behavior. Unless a response was "attached" to a stimulus—that is, unless behavior was observed to change in the presence of a stimulus—it was assumed that no learning had occurred.

Bolles (1975) discusses several conditions under which the correspondence assumption fails to explain the data. Several species of birds, for instance, learn their mating songs only if exposed to them during critical periods of development. However, these species need not actually sing at the time of exposure in order to sing later, sometimes a year hence (Shettleworth, 1972). Domjan and Wilson (1968) have shown that rats can learn an aversion to saccharin even when they are completely paralyzed. And Bandura's research on observational learning (e.g., 1965, 1969, 1977a) shows unequivocally that the acquisition of complex human behavior can occur without immediate behavior change or reinforcement. In these and in other instances, learning occurs in the absence of a specifiable or observably relevant response.

The Universality Assumption

The universality assumption holds that all learning is uniform regardless of species-specific differences or biological influences. The implication of this assumption is that all stimuli and all responses are equally associable. A host of interesting phenomena disclaim such a view. In direct contradiction to established learning parameters, rats can learn taste aversions in one trial even with a conditioned stimulus–unconditioned stimulus (CS–US) delay of an hour or more (Garcia & Koelling, 1966). This "super learning" does not occur if the US is faradic shock rather than illness. A number of species-specific defense and appetitive responses are highly resistant to modification by reinforcement contingencies (Bolles, 1975; Breland & Breland, 1961; Millenson & Leslie 1979; Williams & Williams, 1969). This also points to the fact that learning is not indiscriminate. Lorenz has argued (Bolles, 1975) that organisms respond to the particular aspects of their environment that have been most conducive, in an evolutionary sense, to the survival of their species. Learning, then, is not universally equivalent. It can be highly selective and highly accelerated or constrained according to what Seligman (1971) refers to as "preparedness" of the organism.

The Automaticity Assumption

Skinner (1974) states the automaticity assumption succinctly: "A reinforcer has an effect even though the behavior it follows does not produce it" (p. 134). This simplifying assumption, if viewed as an argument for accidental learning by contiguity (as in superstition), does not adequately explain all the data. Kamin (1969), Maier (1970), Rescorla and Wagner (1972), Watson (1971a, 1971b), and others (see also Schwartz, 1978) have demonstrated that reinforcement in both operant and classical conditioning must usually signal a *contingency* (rather than a contiguity) for behavior to be reliably affected. Learned helplessness (Seligman, 1975), for example, does not result from the superstitious acquisition of passivity, as the automaticity hypothesis would predict (Schwartz, 1978). Instead, as Maier (1970) has shown, it occurs because the subject learns that responding is independent of consequence. If a contingency is added to this experiment so that passivity specifically permits escape from shock, learned helplessness does not occur (Maier, 1970).

Another oversimplification of the automaticity assumption is the notion that reinforcement is a response strengthener. In an intriguing replication of Skinner's (1948) superstition experiment, Staddon and Simmelhag

(1971) showed that reinforcement acts not to strengthen a response but to select it from the existing behavioral repertoire. Selection in their experiment occurred only when a response-dependent contingency was in effect.

Implications

The downfall of the assumptions we have discussed has enormous implications for a theory and therapy of psychological distress. If learning is not necessarily equivalent to performance, then the variance at R cannot always be fully explained by S, and it becomes essential to look inside the "black box" for further information. Mahoney (1974) reviews several learning studies with human subjects in which (1) different responses are made to the same stimulus, (2) identical responses are made to different stimuli, and (3) either the response or the stimulus is impossible to observe. Mediational processes between S and R were inferred to explain these results. Applying this concept to the clinical situation, a student who fails an exam and becomes depressed may benefit by examining his or her *thinking* about failure, as well as by developing improved study skills. A snake phobic entering a zoo may reinterpret experienced anxiety as a "cue to cope" (Meichenbaum, 1977). And a chronic pain patient may ameliorate distress by means of pleasant imagery (Turk, 1978).

The deficiency of the universality assumption is also important in this regard. If all stimuli and all responses are not equally associable, therapists may need to tailor their interventions to some clinical problems and not to others. Cautela's (1967) covert sensitization procedure, for example, seems to have greater efficacy in the treatment of sexual deviations than in the treatment of smoking, obesity, or alcoholism (Mahoney, 1974). Several authors (e.g., Chomsky; 1959; Lenneberg, 1967; Millenson & Leslie, 1979; Seligman, 1970; Slobin, 1971) have argued that human beings are genetically prepared to acquire language. These authors assert that (1) language development occurs very rapidly and at a very early age, (2) language acquisition is extraordinarily systematic, and (3) language consistency occurs despite widely varying environmental influences. Classical conditioning of word meaning occurs readily in human beings (Razran, 1961; Staats, 1968), and negative affect is easily conditioned to verbal cues (Maltzman, 1968; Staats, 1968). These findings give us a clue to the often traumatic nature of human belief in "irrational ideas" (Ellis, 1974), i.e., such ideas predict and elicit negative affect. Since language seems to facilitate conditioned autonomic distress, treatment modes that emphasize cognition in conjunction with conditioning paradigms should be helpful in alleviating such distress. McMullin and Casey's (1975) *voluntary cortical inhibition* (VCI) procedure was designed according to this reasoning and will be explained in later chapters.

Finally, the efficacy of clinical technique may be increased by an understanding of the intricacies of the law of effect. Cautela's covert reinforcement procedure (1970) has not received a great deal of empirical support (Mahoney, 1974) and is a case in point. In this procedure, the client imagines performing a target behavior (e.g., calling someone for a date) and follows this scene with images of reinforcement (e.g., eating an ice cream cone). In studies by Maier (1970), Staddon and Simmelhag (1971), and others, conditioning occurred only when reinforcement provided information about the environment and was dependent, or contingent, upon a response. Cautela's procedure is based on the automaticity assumption and does not take these factors into account. It is hard to see, for example, how eating an ice cream cone relates to calling a person for a date. In line with the contingency hypothesis of learning, we would expect McMullin and Casey's (1975) *self-punishment–self-reward* (SP–SR) technique (discussed later) to show greater efficacy than self-reinforcement because in the SP–SR technique the imagined consequences are more relevant to the response (e.g., "If I can learn to ask people out, I won't be so isolated any more!"). This hypothesis awaits empirical testing. Interestingly, reviews by Brewer (1974) and Bandura (1969) have shown that learning is often facilitated when subjects are made aware of experimental contingencies. These demonstrations again point to the fact that increasing the information about response-dependent consequences facilitates change.

A NEOBEHAVIORIST APPROACH TO COGNITIVE BEHAVIOR THERAPY

Of the three types of behavior therapy listed by Wilson (1978)—applied behavior analysis, neobehaviorist mediational therapy, and social learning therapy—the neobehaviorist approach is most closely related to the cognitive techniques we present. In our techniques, verbal conditioning interventions are directed at mediational cognitions, and mediational constructs, such as situational imagery and thoughts, are assumed to be tied to antecedent and consequent events. It has been our experience that such cognitive restructuring techniques are helpful in and of themselves in alleviating a variety of psychological problems (see Chapter 4). We do not contend, however, that they can or should be used exclusively, that is, in lieu of other techniques. The procedures used to treat a problem should follow a careful assessment of that problem. A fear of flying, for example, may require systematic desensitization, cognitive restructuring, marital counseling, and/or other techniques depending on the nature of the variables involved. The reader is referred to Kanfer and Phillips (1970, p. 54) and to Chapter 3 of this volume for a discussion of the variables included in a behavior assessment.

Consistent with a neobehaviorist philosophy, we propose interventions that are designed primarily to change cognitions. It is assumed that changes in affect and behavior will follow. We should point out, however, that some authors do not agree with this philosophy. Bandura (1977b) argues that changing behavior is the best way to change cognition, because a greater amount of corrective feedback is obtained (i.e., motoric, observational, and affective). Wilson (1978), after reviewing some of the literature on anxiety management, has agreed with Bandura and has recommended using performance based techniques over imaginal or verbal ones.

Although Wilson has addressed this issue cogently, there are several reasons why therapists practicing imaginal and/or verbal techniques should not abandon such techniques as a result of his remarks. First, nearly all the performance-superior studies Wilson reviewed were concerned with anxiety management. Problems such as grief, guilt, anger, and depression have not been fully addressed in the manner of these studies. This point applies to anxiety management as well. Husted (1975), for example, found no significant differences in treatment efficacy between imaginal desensitization and in vivo tasks for sexually dysfunctional women. In Husted's study, both techniques were significantly more effective than controls. Furthermore, significantly fewer sessions were required for improvement in women treated with the cognitive technique (7.8 sessions) than in women treated with the performance-based technique (13.3 sessions).

Second, there are many clinical situations in which direct behavior change is difficult if not impossible to effect. In these instances, a cognitive imaginal procedure often becomes the treatment of choice. The following cases exemplify this dilemma:

- A man with sexual performance anxiety has no current sexual partner, and surrogates are unavailable
- A client who has a phobia of flying cannot afford the expense of in vivo desensitization.
- A woman entering couples' counseling for sexual dysfunction thinks, "I hate my partner and question our relationship's validity" (Steger, 1978, p. 103).

Third, most of the current comparative studies assume that the treatment techniques they discuss were carried out expertly. Since cognitive therapy guidelines with respect to such issues as client preparation, potential resistances, complications in treatment, and number of repetitions needed are either nonexistent or not readily available, the assumption of expertise is questionable. DiLoreto (1971) found that systematic desensitization worked significantly better than RET for extroverted subjects. Critiquing this work, however, Ellis (DiLoreto, 1971), argued that the RET was "watered down"; moreover, he said, the method was too didactic, and the counselors (graduate students) were inadequately trained.

Fourth, any argument for the exclusive superiority of cognitive techniques over behavioral ones (or vice versa) implies a separation between the two that is somewhat artificial. Cognitions can serve as responses, discriminative stimuli, and reinforcers (cf. Mahoney, 1974) and thus are "behaviors" subject to lawful influence. A careful clinical assessment will include a check for mediational contributors, and their direct modification can be used in a supplementary fashion to boost the efficacy of other behavioral techniques (e.g., Steger, 1978).

CONSTRUCTS AS EXPLANATION IN CLINICAL PSYCHOLOGY

The demise of the assumptions discussed in the first major section of this chapter has greatly influenced functional explanations of behavior. It is important to note that the new explanations proposed by learning theorists still relate directly to physical events and physiological processes (see, e.g., Millenson & Leslie, 1978). Researchers in clinical psychology seem less likely to anchor their explanations in such events and processes, and we would caution that when theorizing relies too heavily on indefinite terminology and analogous reasoning, it loses explanatory power. Meichenbaum (1977), for instance, has argued against the counterconditioning explanation of systematic desensitization. But his alternative explanation—that the client is learning "coping skills"—generates as many questions as it answers. Why for example, is the acquisition of coping skills therapeutically effective? Is it classical conditioning, operant conditioning, or something totally different? Although Ellis's contributions to the field (e.g., 1962; 1974) have been invaluable, his semantic theory is also quite difficult to pin down. We beg to differ with philosophical explanations of emotional distress and contend that the trauma elicited by irrational ideas has occurred largely by means of direct or vicarious conditioning. Cognitions such as "I must be perfect," "I'm worthless," and "Everyone must love me," are neither inherently nor invariably painful:

> In a fit of religious fervor, Rabbi Goldstein went to his synagogue one day to pray. With great ardor, he began to shout, "I am nothing—I am nothing!" Two of the rabbi's friends happened to be passing by and, upon hearing his ardent cries, went inside to see what was wrong. Soon, all three were vigorously shouting, "I am nothing!"
>
> As fate would have it, the janitor who was working nearby became so inspired by these proceedings that he joined the threesome and also began shouting, "I am nothing!" with great zeal. The rabbi, however, was disgruntled by this addition, "Humpf!" he snorted to his friend. "Look who thinks he's nothing!"

PART II

Assessment and Evaluation: Intake Sessions

The techniques detailed in this book are not helpful to everyone and work much better for some problems than for others. Therefore, the chapters on assessment and evaluation address the following questions: Can we help the client? Are the techniques we use appropriate to the problem? Is a referral indicated?

Part II describes the techniques we use to assess the intensity and extent of psychological discomfort, as well as to evaluate the specific maladaptive cognitions involved (see also Chapters 6 and 7). We have found these techniques invaluable to our work. However, as far as we know, the techniques we use to assess specific cognitions, e.g., irrational belief inventories, structural questioning (Bandler and Grinder, 1975), self-report from memory, and in vivo thought sampling, have not yet been adequately tested for reliability and validity. This limitation is likely due to the relative newness of cognitive-behavior therapy, as well as to the inherent difficulty of assessing cognitions. Although research is badly needed in this area, much preliminary work has been done, and we refer the reader to Kendall and Korgeski's (1979) review.

3

Initial Contact and Assessment: First Session

The literature on the application of cognitive therapy is truly extensive. Positive results have been reported in the treatment of anxiety, anger, chronic pain, self-control, obesity, sexual dysfunction, depression, and so on (see, e.g., Foreyt & Ranjan, 1978; Kendall & Hollon, 1979). We believe that cognitive therapy is often applied best in conjunction with other techniques (cf. Steger, 1978). However, for purposes of instruction, we present our work as it can be applied clinically to the exclusion of nearly all other procedures (that is, in cases of emotional distress with predominantly cognitive components). In this sense, cognitive restructuring therapy (CRT) cannot help every person or every problem. It seems especially effective (that is, 80–86 percent of clients show significant improvement) in "free-floating" or pervasive anxiety, depression with a strong cognitive component, guilt, obsessional ruminations, specific phobias, agoraphobia, and misattributed distress (e.g., "If I forget something, I must be going crazy"). The authors have also used CRT to supplement other behavior therapy techniques in treating pedophilia and exhibitionism, sexual dysfunction, marital problems, obesity, bulimirexia, obsessive-compulsive disorders, insomnia, hysterical amnesia, and social fears (see Chapter 4 for more information). In general, CRT is extremely helpful in treating neurotic (learned) problems that are caused or exacerbated by maladaptive cognitions. It is not, however, helpful for individuals with deficits in the behavioral repertoire, such as a lack of social skills, or for people who cannot identify their feelings.

Obviously, some assessment procedure must be undertaken to find out whether cognitive restructuring will be helpful to the presenting problem. Since we assume that beliefs are directly observable by the client (e.g., Mahoney, 1974), we expect to gain much of the assessment information through structural questioning in the interview (e.g., Bandler & Grinder, 1975). Several other assessment measures can be used, however, and a few of these are mentioned below. It is important to note in this regard that the literature on cognitive-behavior therapy often suggests that certain techniques can be applied "like medicine" to certain clinical problems. The usual study applies a standard technique to a group of people with a common, "standard" problem and then assesses the result (e.g., Kendall and Hollon, 1979). Since the typical study makes little mention of client preparation, the persuasive influence of "being in an experiment," and handling initial resistances, a clinician reading this work might assume that cognitive techniques are as easy and as simple to apply as a recipe from a cookbook. This is far from the case, as Cameron (1978), in an excellent chapter on cognitive sources of resistance, makes clear. The client usually comes to the therapist with a plethora of beliefs, expectations, feelings, and behaviors about what he or she will be "in for," and these must be effectively addressed for maximum therapeutic results. In the assessment phase, even before we can know whether or not to use CRT, we help our clients to understand our procedures and rationales in preparation for a possible therapeutic contract. How this preparation occurs will be explained below.

THE INITIAL CONTACT

Most of our initial contacts occur by phone. We believe it is important even at this stage to give the potential client an honest idea of what the initial interviews will entail. Therefore, after we have obtained objective data such as name and address, we are likely to say something like the following to the client:

> There are many different therapies available, and I cannot at this point know whether the kind I do will be helpful to you. It usually takes me two sessions to make this decision, and I would ask you to help me by filling out some questionnaires or psychological tests after we meet for the first time. At the second session I will tell you whether or not I think I can be of help. If I

do not think my type of therapy would help you, I will give you a referral to someone else. Is this all right with you?

The above series of statements counters many commonly held beliefs about therapy by implying, "This is not a doctor–patient relationship. The cure will not be magic, and it may entail your doing work outside the office." Therapists say honestly that they will not undertake a case unless they are fairly sure they can help. This approach helps to build trust and has been shown to facilitate attitude change (Walster, Aronson, & Abrahams, 1966). Finally, the client is asked if this procedure meets expectations. We usually explain our methods and techniques first and then ask for permission to use them. If clients say "Yes," their commitment to treatment tends to increase.

THE FIRST SESSION

Clients may appear at the first session with any number of concerns. They may have negative impressions of psychotherapy from friends, family, television, or referral sources and, quite appropriately, enter therapy with some degree of caution (Cameron, 1978). They may fear being labeled or evaluated negatively or that the therapist will "read their minds." Therapists are often portrayed in movies and on television as unscientific "kooks" who do not know what they are doing, and this possibility may add to a client's apprehension. Depressed clients may enter the office thinking their situation is hopeless. Anxious clients may think they are going crazy, and clients referred by the courts may be determined to resist therapeutic efforts in every way. Few clients know a priori how to express their problems in specific terms, and many feel uncomfortable at the thought of talking to a stranger.

Consequently, the first session emphasizes relationship building. The therapist tries to make the situation as relaxed and informal as possible (e.g., Haley, 1976). Statements such as the following are common: "I realize it must be hard trying to talk to a complete stranger"; "You seem a bit nervous. Would you like some water?"; "Do you mind if I smoke?" "Excuse me while I get my matches"; "I'm going to go get a coke. Would you like one?"

After several minutes of such small talk, the therapist reiterates that the purpose of the first session is to find out if the therapy will be appropriate. This gives a rationale for asking questions, which many clients appreciate (Cameron, 1978). We may get a brief case history and inquire about previous therapy, other attempts to solve the problem, and medical complications. If other therapy has not worked, it is important to find out why. Several of our clients who were referred from unsuccessful "cognitive-behavior therapy" were somewhat less than optimistic about this procedure.

Questioning about the specific presenting complaint begins with a restatement of what the client said over the phone. This shows that we have taken time to prepare for the session and that we are not just dealing with client No. 134A. At this point, we ask for more detail about the problem and obtain information sufficient to choose appropriate assessment instruments. This questioning is interspersed with numerous supportive and reflective statements such as "Can you help me with this?"; "I'm wondering what happened *after* you got so anxious"; "That must have been torturous for you."

Assessment instruments are not administered until we tell the client our general hypotheses about the nature of the problem. If the problem seems to be cognitively based anxiety, for instance, we may say something like "Your anxiety could be related to your thoughts about this issue or to the way you perceive the situation." But we don't press the concept. We do not want the client to argue against the "thoughts cause feelings" notion, and it has been our experience that such resistance is much more likely to occur if theory and technique are presented in the absence of a thorough assessment. (The client may think that the problem that may have existed for years is being oversimplified and "packaged" into a stereotyped treatment procedure.)

Assessment instruments are given to the client to fill out at home and return by mail. The client is told that the tests will not reveal so-called hidden material and are used simply to get information without added expense. In addition to information, the tests provide rough baseline data and serve to corroborate our opinions or point to areas of concern we may have missed. The Spielberger State–Trait Anxiety Inventory (1969), Zung's Depression Inventory (1965), the Fear Survey and the Assertion Checklist (Wolpe, 1969), or the Irrational Belief Questionnaire (Casey & McMullin, 1976), may be given depending on the nature of the problem. Author McMullin uses the Minnesota Multiphasic Personality Inventory with many clients, and author Giles uses the Life History Questionnaire (Wolpe, 1973), the Willoughby Personality Scale (Wolpe, 1973), and the Beck Depression Inventory (Beck, Rush, Shaw, & Emery, 1979). We emphasize that all the tests are given to assess specific behaviors and specific cognitions in situations and not, therefore, to assess global "personality traits." Most clients feel that their problems have been given careful scrutiny as a result of these procedures, and they are likely to cooperate with subsequent interventions. The results of the tests help stimulate more specific questioning about the nature of the clients' problems, and we explain the results thoroughly to clients (as promised) at the second session.

Many of our clients want to make a therapeutic contract after the first meeting and ask if we will accept them for treatment. We defer our answer to the second session with the explanation that we want to be as certain as possible we can help before agreeing to a contract. The decision to enter into a therapeutic contract is made on the basis of the assessment. Further information about this process is provided in the next chapter.

4

Evaluation: Second Session

During the interim between the first and second evaluation sessions, the therapist reviews the returned test information and hypothesizes about contributors to the problem. In this way, the therapist forms an opinion as to whether or not the cognitive restructuring approach would be appropriate. Ideal CRT clients are of average or above average intelligence, and their psychological distress is not severely disruptive. CRT may be somewhat useful for psychotic patients, although it cannot be used to cure them; CRT also cannot be used initially in severe depression that can be ameliorated only with antidepressant medication. In such instances, we refer clients to a psychiatrist. Because we do not have a complete 24-hour emergency service, we may refer clients who appear acutely suicidal to the nearest mental health center. We have also referred to other facilities clients who stated (and demonstrated) a strong reluctance to do outside work on their problems.

Interestingly, CRT is often helpful only when a client's level of anxiety, depression, or other indicators of distress (as measured by self-report and by assessment instruments) falls within a moderate-to-high-discomfort range. People who are not very distressed usually lack the motivation to do the homework. As stated earlier, CRT is not the treatment of choice for behavioral problems, such as lack of specific assertiveness skills or tendency to have negative social interactions, and its therapeutic potential is limited when environmental conditions are overwhelmingly noxious. Author Giles, for instance, had a client who in a span of six weeks had surgery on his foot, was hospitalized twice for medical emergencies, lost his apartment belongings in a robbery, was sued for divorce, temporarily lost his job, and filed for bankruptcy.

DETERMINING APPROPRIATE THERAPY

It should be evident from this discussion that cognitive restructuring in and of itself does not have unlimited applicability and often must be supplemented or replaced with other techniques. Client characteristics for maximum success with CRT include:

- Of average to above-average intelligence
- Not in an acute crisis state
- Feeling moderate to high levels of functional distress
- Able to identify feelings
- Not psychotic or severely debilitated by the problem
- Willing to do the homework
- Able to call upon an adequate behavioral repertoire

On the basis of the foregoing criteria, approximately 30 percent of our clientele are not suitable for a primarily CRT approach. The percentage of unsuitable clients will vary, of course, according to the population served.

Since the assessment decision is so crucial to later success, we will illustrate it further with some modified case examples. In order to help the reader follow the way in which different factors are weighed, each of these cases is outlined according to Kanfer and Phillip's (1970) SORKC model where

S = situational influences
O = biological state of the organism (including all effects from regular medications as well as psychotropic drugs)
R = responses (including thoughts and feelings)
K = contingency
C = consequence (reinforcer)

Case 1: Mary T.
Presenting Problem: Forty Pounds Overweight

S: Mary's excess eating occurred between 8:30 and 10:00 P.M. every night while she watched television.

O: Mary exercised very infrequently; consequently, calories were burned inefficiently, and less muscle tissue was available to speed calorie loss (Bailey, 1978). A physical examination revealed no evidence of hypothyroidism, adrenal tumor, incipient diabetes, or other organic factors.

R—Behavior: Mary ate an average of 1500 calories of potato chips, candy, and other high-calorie snacks while watching television.

R—Thoughts: "I have no willpower. I promised myself I would never overeat again. What's the use of trying?"

R—Feelings: Hopelessness, guilt

K: Continuous schedule

C: Besides the obvious payoff of food, this variable was not completely determined at the initial assessment. Mary scored high on the Social Introversion scale of the MMPI, and her Assertion measures were low for social interaction. Consequently, it is possible that she felt somewhat anxious about social contacts and avoided them by staying home in the evenings.

Mary T. was not a good candidate for a strictly CRT approach. Outside the "cognitive claustrophobia" (see Mahoney & Mahoney, 1976) evidenced above, she seemed to have a minimum of contributing maladaptive thoughts, and her test scores did not indicate a significant amount of emotional distress. Most of her problem was situationally controlled and behaviorally based, so that any number of the techniques now available for weight control, such as stimulus-control and self-monitoring, could have been applied appropriately (e.g., Abramson, 1976; Mahoney & Mahoney, 1976; Nash & Long, 1978; Stuart & Davis, 1972). Mary was referred to a behavioral weight-loss clinic in order to save her expense.

Case 2: Fred J.
Presenting Problem: Dating Anxiety

S: Parties, singles bars, and the like where Fred had the opportunity to meet single women.

O: Relevance not apparent

R—Behaviors: Social withdrawal or literal escape from the situation. When Fred did attempt to meet someone, he stumbled over his words and was unable to think of much to say.

R—Thoughts: "God, it would be horrible if I asked someone to dance and she refused. What a fool I would be! That would prove I'm inferior to other men. I'd be better off to just get out of here."

R—Feelings: Anxiety, inadequacy, confusion

K: Continuous

C: Avoidance of social anxiety

Fred J., was a good candidate for CRT. As reflected in the Willoughby test, Wolpe's assertion checklist, and interview data, Fred had a number of maladaptive cognitions about his sense of self worth and felt strong anxiety in social situations. He had never had a chance to learn effective social skills, and as a result such skills were lacking in his behavioral repertoire. Consequently, social skills and assertiveness training were used in conjunction with the CRT approach.

Case 3: Diane K.
Presenting Problem: Feelings of Worthlessness and Inadequacy

S: (1) Diane's supervisor at work failed to appear at meetings that Diane had scheduled; (2) Her husband, a lawyer, used complex words in their conversations. Diane often did not understand what he was saying.

O: Relevance not apparent

R—Behaviors: (1) Diane either said nothing to her supervisor or asked if he would like to reschedule the meeting; (2) Diane angrily and sulkily told her husband that he did not understand her.

R—Thoughts: (1) "He is deliberately missing these meetings with me. I must not be worth talking to. Nothing ever works out! It's just like a man. Women don't have a chance in this society. I should tell him my feelings, but I'm afraid of creating a scene and being a bitch. What an utter, incredible worm I am." (2) "If I don't understand all of his big words, I must be stupid. It's awful to be stupid, and it's his fault for making me feel this way. What a bastard!"

R—Feelings: Hopelessness, anger, inadequacy

K: Intermittent schedule

C: Sometimes Diane withdrew from the situation, feeling miserable about herself. At other times, she "blew her stack" and got temporary respite from the noxious elements in her environment.

Diane K.'s case was quite suitable for a CRT approach. Questioning, role-playing, and other techniques showed that Diane knew appropriate behavioral responses in various situations but was afraid to use them due to her inaccurate cognitions (e.g., "Speaking up to the boss is being a bitch, and being a bitch is horrible"; "I'm stupid and worthless if I don't understand every word spoken in every conversation with my husband"). Therapeutic interventions were directed at the modification of Diane's intervening cognitions.

The cases we have discussed were very clear-cut and have been further simplified here for illustrative purposes. Many other presenting problems, although especially appropriate for CRT, are maintained by cognitions whose range of influence is extraordinarily more extensive, subtle, and complex. Assessment questions and procedures concerning the use of CRT remain essentially the same in these cases. Once CRT is deemed appropriate, however, extensive assessment of the cognitions themselves is necessary by means of more advanced procedures. These procedures will be explained in later chapters.

CONVEYING ASSESSMENT INFORMATION TO THE CLIENT

At the beginning of the second evaluation session, we explain the results of all our tests and interview data fully to the client. Clients are usually impressed that we can learn so much about them from the tests and from one interview. And the client's perception of our expertise tends to facilitate later attitude change (Aronson, 1972; Hovland & Weiss, 1951). In addition, the tests allow some degree of evaluative distancing, thereby removing the therapist from a blaming position (e.g., "These tests show [rather than "I think"] that you feel terribly anxious in a lot of situations, so perhaps we could start working on that"). If our assessment shows that someone else could help the client more effectively or with less expense, we explain this and make the referral. Otherwise, clients are told what they can expect from the therapy, what the probability of success is, what we will expect from them, etc. For example:

> You have what is known as agoraphobia. I'm sure your problem seems very confusing to you now, but we will in all likelihood find that you feel this way for understandable reasons. These reasons probably involve the way you think about certain things, but we will get to that next week if you decide to continue.
>
> Before you make this decision, there are several things you should know. First, the therapy takes approximately 15 weeks, one hour a week, and I will expect you to do up to two hours of homework per week. If you do not do this, the treatment will not work. Second, you will not feel any better for at least another five weeks because the techniques used to change painful feelings take several weeks of careful preparation. If I could help you sooner, I would. But I have tried to skip the preliminaries before, and my success rate fell to 50 percent. I have an 86 percent success rate with this problem. How does this seem to you?

This series of statements accomplishes several objectives:

1. It states the "thoughts cause feelings" notion in general terms.
2. It gives the client an estimate of the length of treatment and probability of success.
3. It emphasizes the gradual process of improvement and thus counters the common expectation of a magic cure, setting the expectation of immediate relief at a very low probability. Usually, however, owing to the "nonspecific" factors in psychotherapy, clients begin to feel better anyway and believe the therapy is working especially well for them.
4. It makes clear the necessity for outside work.

We do not accept a contract from clients at this point. We want them to make this decision only after thinking about it carefully in a context divorced from our direct influence. If a client calls later in the week to accept treatment (almost all do), such an active step towards the therapy is very likely to increase his or her sense of commitment (e.g., Linder, Cooper, & Jones, 1967).

For homework, clients are asked to do the following:

- List in a notebook the 10 worst things that have happened to them in their adult lives.
- Bring the notebook to the next session.

PART III

Cognitive Restructuring Therapy: Identifying and Analyzing Cognitions

It has been our experience that clients must be taught several specific skills before direct cognitive-change interventions are employed. As the next few chapters will make clear, we usually spend five sessions teaching these skills, but some clients may require more. We have found these skills indispensable.

5

Teaching the Concepts: First Therapy Session

The first phase of stress-inoculation training is designed to provide the client with a conceptual framework, in *lay terms,* for understanding the nature of his response to stressful events. The most important aspect of this phase is that the conceptual framework should be plausible to the client and its acceptance should naturally lead to the practice of specific, cognitive, and behavioral coping techniques. Thus, the logic of the training regimen becomes more comprehensible to a client in light of the conceptualization offered.

It should be underscored that the scientific validity of a particular conceptualization is less crucial than its face validity or air of plausibility for the client . . . . Naturally, any conceptualization must be offered with clinical sensitivity. The purpose of providing a framework is not to convince the client—perhaps against his will—that any particular explanation of his problem is valid but rather to encourage him to view his problem from a particular perspective and thus accept and collaborate in the therapy that will follow.

Indeed, I will argue . . . that therapists, and behavior therapists in particular, have failed to pay sufficient attention to the initial conceptualization phase of therapy. What transpires be-

> tween client and therapist prior to the implementation of specific treatment procedures plays an important role in understanding the change process.*

We fully agree with Meichenbaum's position and devote an entire session with the client to the conceptualization of our therapy. Most clients' primary cognition is that everything *but* their thinking is causing the problem: It is their mother, father, childhood, repressed libido, or problems at home. Only very rarely does someone say, "Help me change these nutty thoughts!"

The client must be shown, therefore, how thinking is tied to feelings and behaviors, and we devote the first session to this endeavor. At the beginning of the interview we say,

> I will mainly lecture to you today so that you will have a better understanding of the theory from which I work. At the end of the session, you will probably also have a better understanding of your problems, but I want you to know that we will not be working directly on them until later, okay? Do you understand?

After securing an agreement to proceed, we begin with an elucidation of other theories of behavior. Each is briefly and generally explained, and each is shown to have certain limitations. We make sure to include any theories in which the client might believe. (The client is never asked to state these, so we guess at these theories from information obtained in the interview.) If we suspect a client is blaming his or her childhood, for instance, we would say the following:

> Several theorists believe that all problems come from traumatic events in childhood. In fact, this view dominated psychology for a number of years. Of course, something that happened in the past cannot affect us unless it is still being "carried around" in the present in some way. The best therapy, then, is one that finds exactly how the problem is manifested in the present so that it can be changed directly.

If a client has had psychoanalytic treatment, we will go into some detail about this theory and explain how our approach differs. And we may ask the client if he or she has ever known someone who understood the

---

*From *Cognitive-Behavior Modification* by D. Meichenbaum. New York: Plenum, 1977, pp. 150–151. Copyright by Plenum Press. Reprinted by permission.

origin of a problem but was not subsequently relieved of it. (Some clients can give numerous examples.)

It is crucial to note that never during this discourse is the client implicated directly. We show that we understand several points of view without making him or her "own" any of them. Thus the client can save face when we refute these theories and promote our own. The reader may note quite a contrast between Ellis's approach and this one. We do not wait for the client to state his or her position publicly so that we can then destroy it. Instead the client sees how other people may be mistaken and thus is allowed to join us tacitly and without confrontation. The social psychological literature has shown this procedure to facilitate attitude change (Sherif & Hovland, 1961).

The situation-causes-response theory is always brought up last and refuted in some detail. This gives us an opportunity to explain A–B–C terminology (Ellis, 1962), as well as to challenge a popularly held theory of behavior. For example:

> The last theory I want to tell you about is the A causes C theory. "A" stands for the situation. I would like you to write that down in your notebook. Formally, it stands for "antecedent event," but all you have to know is that it means "situation." The "C" stands for the consequence; that is, feelings or behavior. How about writing that down, too? Now, most people think that A causes C. For example, if they went to a funny movie and were asked what made them laugh, they would say that the *movie* did. The movie is the A, and the laughter is the C. Or, if an employee got angry because his boss yelled at him, most people would say that the boss's yelling made the employee mad. In this case, the yelling would be the A and the anger would be the C. Although events or situations can sometimes cause feelings, a lot of the time they do not. Feelings and behaviors are most often caused by beliefs or "Bs."

The client is told that beliefs can be superstitions, images, values, thoughts, expectations, perceptions, anticipations, words, sentences, themes, or even whole philosophies. Then, the client is given several examples in which the consequences seem caused by the beliefs:

> I had a client once whose five-year-old son used to come into her bedroom twice a month crying. We found out that the moonlight at these times formed a shadow in the boy's room that

> looked like a wolf. Now, obviously it was not really a wolf that caused the fear, and it wasn't the shadow either because shadows don't cause emotions. It had to be what the boy was *saying to himself* about the shadow; for example, "It's a wolf and it will hurt me!"
>
> When my daughter was three, she used to watch monster shows on TV and get scared. When she was five, she watched the same shows and laughed like crazy. The situations were the same, but the consequences were different. Why do you think this was so?
>
> A New Yorker went to Texas to visit his friend. As they were driving in the desert, the New Yorker spotted what he thought was a boulder in the road and frantically tried to grab the wheel. The Texan, however, said, "Relax. It's just a mesquite bush." Do you see how it was what the New Yorker *thought* about the bush that caused his panic? (Snygg & Combs, 1949).
>
> Two men overate one night and woke up the next morning feeling sick. One went to the doctor in a panic and the other simply took it easy until he felt better. The first man was saying something pretty scary to himself. What do you think that might have been?

Although the presentation up to this point can be read very quickly, it usually takes 20 minutes or more to complete. We are collaborating with the client and trying to elicit his or her active participation.

After clients have heard the examples above, they may be asked to close their eyes and imagine some pleasant scene; for example, lying on a beach or getting presents when they were children. Clients usually report feeling happy and relaxed, and we point out that their *imagination* of the event has caused their feelings, since the event itself was not present.

The client is then presented with a series of examples in which the same A leads to different Bs and thus to different Cs. For example, we may say,

> Okay, now remember that situation where the boss gets upset and starts yelling at his employee? That's the A. Now if the employee were to think, "That son of a bitch has his nerve yelling at me! I don't have to stand for this!" and so on, what would his C be? Right! His C would be anger. But suppose he were to think, "Oh God! He is yelling at me again. I can't do

> anything right. How wretched I am! I should be chopped up and used for fertilizer" and so forth. What would his C be then? Yeah, he would be awfully depressed, wouldn't he?

We usually follow with several A–C situations and have the client guess the Bs. A number of such examples can be found in McMullin and Casey (1975). If time permits, other techniques that explain A–B–C theory further are used at this point. The client may be asked to give an example of how a belief affects the behavior or feeling of an acquaintance. Or we may ask the client for a superstition he or she had as a child but no longer believes as an adult. For clients interested in research, we explain recent cognitive experimentation in psychology (e.g., Meichenbaum, 1977) or in neurophysiology. For instance, very recent research using radioisotopes with brain surgery patients (Lasser, Ingvar, & Skinhoj, 1978), has shown that the frontal lobe and cortical areas are activated when anxiety is experimentally induced. We explain how such research supports the mediational hypothesis and then see if the client has any questions.

When the presentation is complete, we ask the $64 question: "Do you think your problem could be due to your beliefs?" At this point, it is unusual for a client to say, "No. I don't think so." (This happens about once in a hundred times.) We ask a client who does say this to hold our B-causes-C premise tentatively until more evidence can be gathered. Almost all clients have a better understanding of their problems at this point and want to continue. We then say,

> The next two sessions will be spent in finding the Bs followed by one or two sessions to determine whether or not these Bs are true. The rest of the treatment will be directed at changing unrealistic beliefs so that you can feel better. You should feel better by the seventh week. Is this all right with you?

This session is brought to a close with a discussion of *sabotages:* "Approximately one person in ten fails to benefit from this approach for reasons that I call 'sabotages.' Sabotages usually occur because of Bs, too. I will give you examples of the most common sabotages so that you will be more able to avoid them."

There is another rationale for discussing sabotages in addition to making clients more aware of them. Most people fail in cognitive restructuring therapy for reasons generally classified as *issues of control* (see Haley, 1963). The maladaptive behaviors spawned by control issues can sometimes be prevented if they are predicted before they occur (Giles, 1979)

The discussion of sabotages predicts the way a person can fail and thus makes clients who have a tendency to "control" by using sabotages less likely to use such measures. We present a more specific definition of "control" and discuss additional ways to handle it in Chapter 12.

The most common sabotages are:

- Failing to do the homework
- Covertly countering most of what the therapist has to say
- Thinking of all problems at once instead of tackling one at a time
- Denying improvement
- Refusing to believe the therapy can work
- Doing the homework incorrectly or half-heartedly
- Refusing to keep trying

We explain these foregoing maneuvers to the client and say, "Of course, these are only the most common sabotages and don't include all possible ploys. If you were going to sabotage the treatment but were afraid to tell me, what would you be likely to do?" Interestingly, clients have often known how they would sabotage treatment—for example, "I would agree with everything you said, and then I would forget about it"—and getting sabotages out in the open has helped us prevent several treatment failures. We end the session by giving the client a homework assignment.

After the first CRT session we ask clients to do the following homework:

- List the worst A–C situation they have every day the following week and bring it in at the next session.
- Buy Albert Ellis's *A New Guide to Rational Living* and read the first two chapters.
- Read to page 17 in *Talk Sense to Yourself*. (This is McMullin's and Casey's 1975 book which we give to every client. In order to help prevent "countering," we ask clients not to read advanced sections until the corresponding techniques have been explained.)

It is important to note that we frequently emphasize to clients the necessity of doing the homework. In most cases, we make it clear that we cannot continue with the next week's plan unless the requisite homework has been done. We always try to respond to completed assignments with ample praise and appreciation.

6
Finding Specific Cognitions: Second Therapy Session

The second cognitive restructuring therapy session is used to assess particular beliefs as they are associated with feelings, behaviors, and other beliefs. At the therapist's disposal are the 10 worst A–C situations the client has had as an adult and the seven worst A–C situations he or she has had for the previous week.

As with most sessions, we begin by reviewing what occurred at the previous interview and explaining what will happen at the present one. Usually, clients want to begin by telling us about their week. We set aside the first 10 to 15 minutes of the interview for this purpose and tie in the A–B–C framework where appropriate (in the order of situation–belief–feeling). Of course, if the client is acutely upset over something, we will drop our agenda and deal with the issue at hand.

After we hear what the client has to say, we are ready to begin the assessment of particular beliefs. This step is crucially important to treatment outcome and will be discussed in some detail.

The client is presented with a list of 45 beliefs that often contribute to emotional problems (see Appendix A). We have compiled this list from our own experience and from that of other clinicians around the country. Using a variation of Beck's (1976) distancing technique, we ask the client to pick one belief from the list—for example, "People must love me or I will be miserable"—and imagine that it is "injected" into the head of a passerby. The client is then asked to state how this person would be affected by the new belief.

The distancing technique allows the client enough objectivity to examine the consequences of particular Bs closely. When CRT was first being developed, clients were asked how they were personally affected by one or another of these cognitions. This would usually lead to a debate; that is, the client would either deny that he or she had such beliefs or would begin arguing for their validity. Now that the client does not have to claim cognitive ownership we almost never encounter this problem.

From 5 to 10 of the beliefs listed in Appendix A are discussed in this fashion, depending on the client's interest. The therapist chooses a few of them, and the client chooses the rest. The cognitions chosen by the therapist resemble those that contribute to the client's problem (although they are still discussed as if they belonged to somebody else). In this manner, the client's responses are shaped so that the transition to personal issues will be easier for him or her to make.

Only after the above preparation is attention shifted to the client's own beliefs. We review the seven A–C situations of the past week and begin exploring for mediational cognitions. This process is done gently. We do not label any beliefs as irrational, crazy, incorrect, or stupid, and we encourage the client as well to refrain from labeling beliefs. By this time clients have heard (several times) that they have acquired certain beliefs as a result of their experiences, that nearly anyone else having these experiences would think the same way, and that everyone has certain beliefs that are not terribly productive. It has been our experience that many people seeking therapy suffer from "I must be perfect" cognitions and that such ideation contributes to the initial resistance that many rational-emotive therapists describe (we elaborate this point in Chapter 8). The strategy delineated above tends to undercut such misery because clients' experiences are implicated but never the clients themselves.

The actual assessment phase begins with one A–C situation at a time. We ask clients to remember what they might have been thinking in each situation and to say whatever comes to mind (Hollon & Beck, 1979). We emphasize that we are searching for the thoughts but that we are not trying to change them. This is a process of investigation, and we assist the client with guesses of our own. We also have the client consider the question of which beliefs from the list could have been elicited in the situation. This process continues as long as time permits or A–C situations remain.

The means by which beliefs are discovered is also quite important. Cognitions seem to interact with each other across meaningful boundaries. Consequently, it is necessary to assess their interconnections so that general patterns of thought can be determined. Structural questioning (see

Bandler & Grinder, 1975) is most useful in this regard and is illustrated with one of our clients below.

A–C Incident No. 1

A: Our client Diane K. tells her supervisor that she is looking for other work; C: anxiety.

Therapist: Okay. You were feeling pretty scared, then, weren't you?
Diane K. Yeah.
T: What might you have been thinking?
D: That he would sabotage me at work.
T: Sabotage? You mean fire you?
D: Yeah.
T: And if he did, what would that mean?
D: I'd have less options.
T: And if you had less options?
D: That would show that I don't know exactly what my career is going to be. My dad told me always to know.
T: There would be some problem with not knowing?
D: Well, then I'd be doing something inadequate again.
T: How do you feel when you do something inadequate?
D: That I'm worthless.
T: Okay, now. Let me see if I've got this. Correct me if I'm wrong. It seems as though you're saying to yourself something like this: "I have to know what I'm going to do with my career, or I will be doing something inadequate again. If I do something inadequate, then I'm worthless." Is that it? Okay. How about writing those beliefs down in your notebook.

A–C Incident No. 2

A: The client is waiting for guests she has invited to her party; C: anxiety.

Therapist: What was anxiety-provoking about waiting for the guests?
Client: I was afraid that no one would show up.
T: What would that mean?
C: That they thought there was something wrong with me.

T: And if they did?
C: Then I guess it would be true.
T: Oh, I see. Are you saying that if someone evaluates you negatively, then you usually think they are right?
C: Yeah. Damn it. I'm so vulnerable to that kind of thing. I just fall apart.
T: You're vulnerable to the criticisms of others because you then begin to criticize yourself. Their criticisms automatically seem true. Why do you think this is so?
C: I don't know. I guess because I have such a low opinion of myself.

A–C Incident No. 3

A: The client's supervisor does not show up for a meeting; C: feelings of worthlessness and inadequacy.

Therapist: What were you thinking when he didn't show up?
Client: That he is a real bastard. It's just like a man.
T: To what?
C: To put a woman down.
T: He put you down by forgetting the meeting?
C: Yeah.
T: What did that say to you?
C: He doesn't think I'm worth talking to.
T: And if he doesn't?
C: Then I must not be.
T: I see. It's the "What other people think makes it so" belief. If you're not worth talking to, then——?
C: Then I'm worthless.

As illustrated above, three seemingly unrelated incidents are connected through meaningful cognitive abstractions to a general devaluation of self-worth. The "I'm worthless" cognition is a *core* belief (McMullin, Assafi, & Chapman, 1978), interacting with a series of other thoughts. On the average, clients have two to four *cores* that become the principal targets of intervention once the assessment phase is complete. This process is discussed further in the next chapter.

Each client forms a master list of Bs by writing them down (as discovered) in the notebook. This process is labeled as exploratory and nonevaluative. Fifteen beliefs are usually discovered in this manner before the session is over.

For homework, the client is asked to do the following:

- Continue the objective review by considering how another person would be affected by five more of the beliefs on the list.
- Find the Bs for any remaining A–C situations and write them in the notebook.
- Continue the A–C exercise for the coming week and add the connecting beliefs.
- Continue reading Ellis until finished. (The client is asked to read no further in McMullin and Casey.)

Homework continues to be of great importance, and we do several things to help clients complete their assignments. First, we explain that the major sabotage at this point is for people to think, "I really know this stuff so I don't have to work very hard." We make it clear that there is still a long way to go and that homework is crucial to later success. If clients do not do their homework at this stage, success rates drop to 50 percent. (This is because such clients tend not to do the cognitive-change homework later.) Second, we ask clients to bring in their weekly schedules so that time for homework can be included and planned for in advance. This step is also helpful as a limiting factor for clients who would otherwise tend to do too much.

7

Continuing to Explore Specific Cognitions

The material in this chapter is usually presented to clients at the third cognitive restructuring therapy session. This schedule is by no means rigid, however, and it may be hastened or delayed according to the requirements of a specific case. Therapist preparation for this session involves consideration and analysis of the presented cognitions so that general patterns of thought can be deduced. For clients whose maladaptive cognitions are few in number and clearly delineated, the material in this chapter can be skipped or given light attention. It has been our experience, however, that cognitive simplicity is more the exception than the rule. Cases of free-floating anxiety sometimes have contributing cognitions numbering in the hundreds, and it was from such clinical complexities that the techniques we will explain shortly were derived. These techniques provide an organization and a uniformity to what might otherwise be overwhelming amounts of cognitive data. Thus large numbers of contributing beliefs can be countered at once.

Inasmuch as 24 A–C situations are at the therapist's disposal, a fairly good review of the client's emotional patterns can be made. Interestingly, the therapeutic structure imposed on this abundance of information often throws a different light on the presenting complaint. It may become clear, for example, that what was presented as depression is actually secondary to anxiety; in such a case anxiety and its antecedents will become the principal targets of intervention.

We have mentioned that assessment concerns the identification of patterns of thought logically connected, across various situations, to a common cognitive element. Diane K., for instance, discussed in the last chapter consistently attributed self-worthlessness to herself in the context of several different A–C events.

An experimental analogue of this process can be found in Razran's (1961) excellent review of Russian conditioning research. For example, in one experiment subjects who knew both Russian and English were conditioned to salivate to the Russian word *dom* (meaning "house"). They were then presented with a CS that was similar either in structure—*dym,* the Russian word for "smoke"—or in meaning—the English word *house. House* elicited significantly more saliva than *dym,* showing that higher-order mediation of word meaning can greatly influence the conditioning process.

Accordingly, beliefs such as "My boss is a son of a bitch," "My guests might not show up," "I'll have fewer career options if I'm fired," and "It's just like a man to put a woman down," although seemingly diverse, can all elicit negative affect by means of conditioning to a common, rudimentary thought (i.e., "I'm worthless"). We regard such *surface* beliefs as stimuli on a generalization gradient. The intensity of the effect each elicits is proportional to its meaningful resemblance to the *core* belief.

This theoretical view suggests an intervention strategy for clinical cases that involve numerous and complex maladaptive cognitions: find the core as it relates to each series of A–C events and extinguish, or countercondition, the affect it elicits. A simultaneous decay of the affect conditioned to all meaningfully related cognitions should occur.

We explain this view carefully to clients by analogy. For example, Diane K., whose beliefs were discussed previously, was told that she possessed a kind of "worthlessness detector" that fired when an event in her environment suggested an inadequacy in her functioning. The therapist explained that her surface Bs were connections between the event and the detector and described them as (1) similar to the bumpers on a pin-ball machine; "You hit any one of them, and the whole board lights up"; and (2) "Like the tentacles of a jellyfish—you get a sting regardless of which one is pulled."

The interconnection of Bs is further illustrated for clients by the *cognitive map* technique whereby the beliefs in several A–C situations are traced to their core. This technique is illustrated with several core Bs in Figures 7–1, 7–2, and 7–3.

We usually find that the cognitive map technique relieves some of the

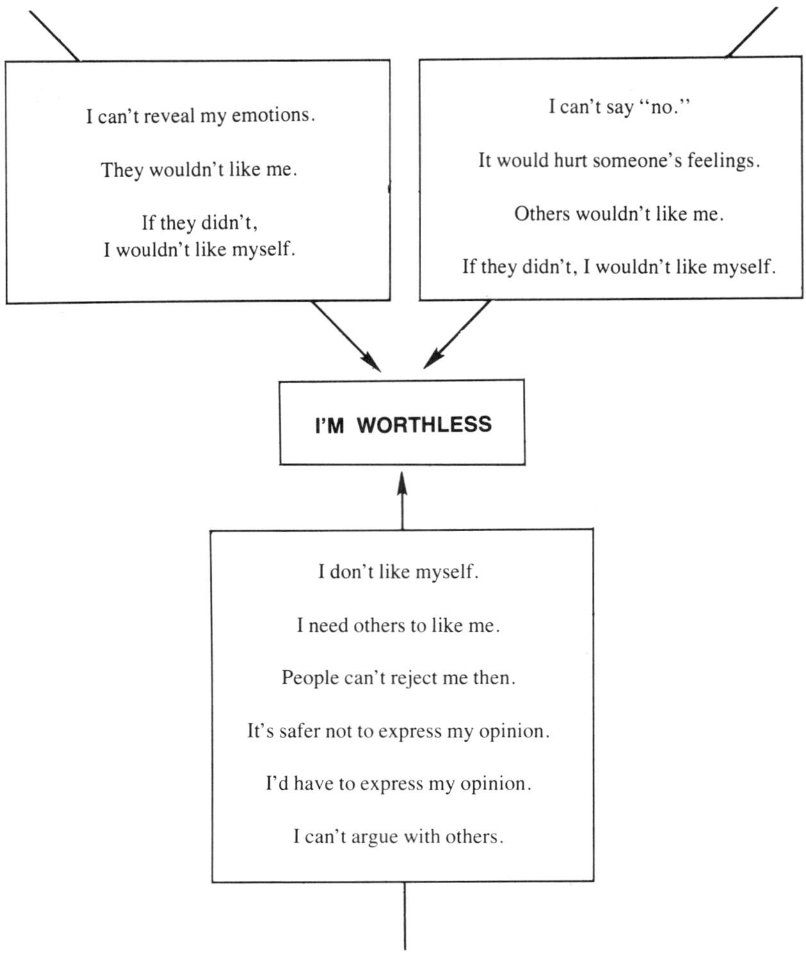

Fig. 7–1. Core belief in self-worthlessness.

client's confusion and anxiety about his or her presenting complaints. It provides a simplifying structure and an observable avenue for change. If the complexities of a case warrant use of the cognitive map, we strongly recommend that assessment continue until the appropriate core beliefs are obtained (even if this takes an additional session). Otherwise, the therapist can easily be sidetracked to extraneous, irrelevant, or noncontributing thoughts, thereby losing the psychological forest among the trees.

Ellis (1978) has observed that clients often potentiate the affective

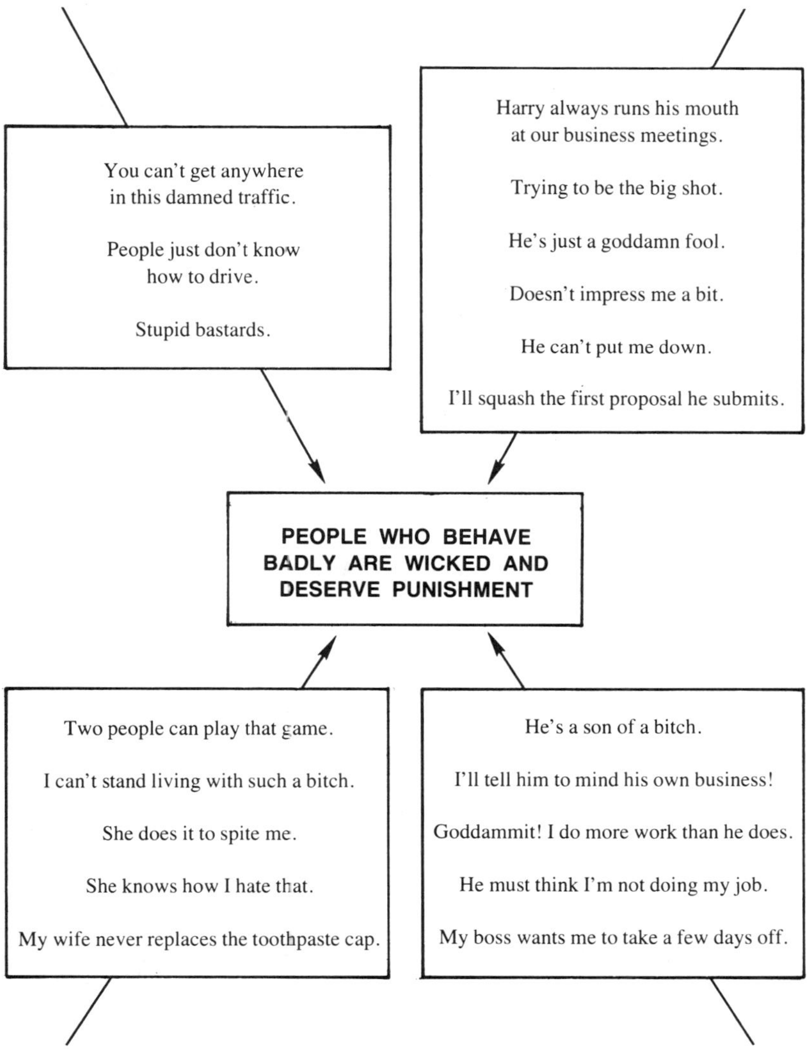

Fig. 7–2. Core belief in wickedness and need for punishment.

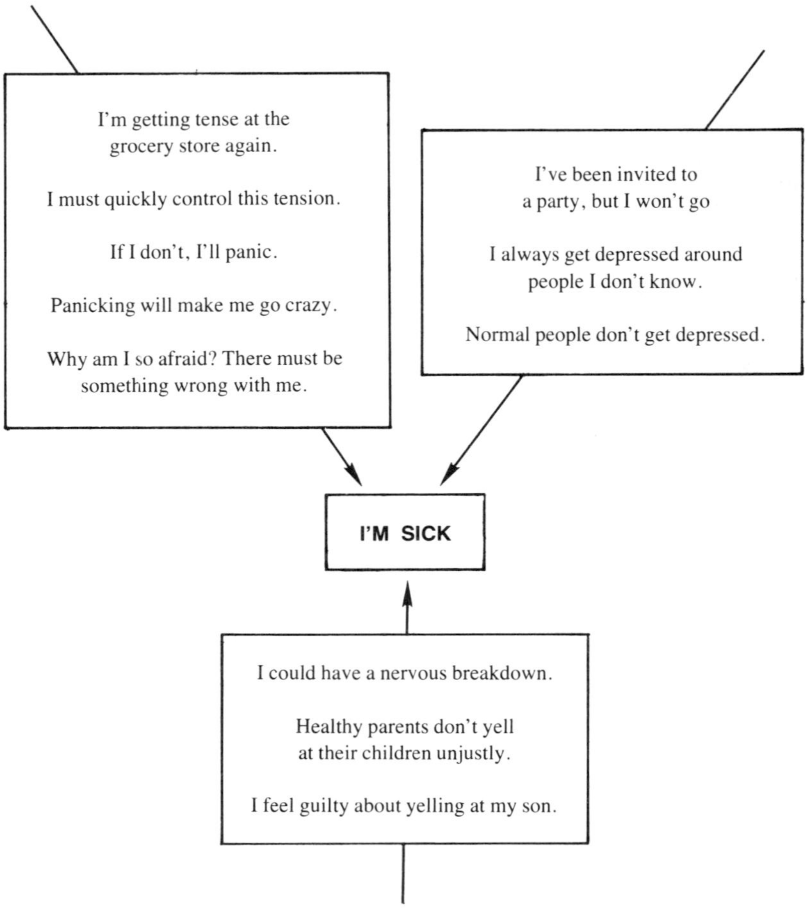

Fig. 7–3. Core belief in one's own "sickness."

misery of their complaints by ruminating maladaptively over them. Thus, some people feel worthless about feeling worthless, anxious about feeling anxious, etc. Our own observations have concurred with Ellis's and we incorporate such ruminations into the cognitive map and cognitive treatment plan when appropriate (e.g., "I feel worthless—I shouldn't feel this way—People should be able to solve their own problems—I can't solve my problems—I really stink"). The distancing technique (see Chapter 6) and the client's contradictory experiences help counter such thoughts in an implicit fashion, and we may counter them explicitly in two ways. First, we may joke with the client about the complaint so that it seems like an accomplishment. For example we may say, "After two weeks of extensive assessment of your Bs, I have some good news. You have one of the best developed 'worthlessness detectors' I've ever seen. I would be very proud if I were you." Second, we may lead the client through a formal exercise that demonstrates the effects of certain self-labels and the arbitrary nature of their selection:

> **Therapist:** We have a few minutes left so I want to go through a word exercise with you. You see, Bs can be single words as well as sentences, expectations, and the like. Some words tend to make us feel good, and others tend to make us feel bad. For example, you can describe, in one word, people who are constantly changing their minds?
> **Client:** Wishy-washy.
> **T:** That word brings up kind of a negative feeling, doesn't it? Can you describe the same sort of people with a positive word?
> **C:** Flexible.
> **T:** Good. Now, how about people who frequently speaks their minds at meetings?
> **C:** Bossy.
> **T:** And a positive?
> **C:** Assertive.
> **T:** Which of these labels is the right one?
> **C:** Well, I really can't say.
> **T:** Right. It's like trying to decide whether a glass is half-empty or half-full. One term is more optimistic than the other. Take your core B, "I'm excitable," for example. Can you think of a positive word for "excitable"?
> **C:** Sensitive—enthusiastic!
> **T:** Yes! An eccentric friend of mine is a master of this process. People are constantly calling him weird. He says, "Thank you. It's one of my best qualities."

This exercise provides a good lead-in to the next topic, *logical analysis*, in which clients learn to view their beliefs from a different perspective (see Chapter 8).

For homework, clients are asked to do the following:

- Continue the A–C exercise and trace the Bs to their core(s).
- Add these to the cognitive map in the notebook.

This chapter ends our formal search for client's Bs. This search, however, continues as long as the client remains in treatment. We are constantly looking for cognitions that might contribute to the success or failure of the therapy. We often get clues to this process from the second part of the homework assignment given above. If a client cannot trace a particular A–C incident to one of his or her known cores, we begin looking for other thoughts that might have escaped previous detection.

8
Logical Analysis

> His [Ellis's] approach is forcefully didactic—so forceful, that on one occasion I was moved to suggest, rather tongue in cheek, that RET as conducted by Ellis would only be successful with New Yorkers (Meichenbaum, 1977, p. 190).

In the foregoing passage, Meichenbaum is referring to Ellis's confrontational therapeutic style, which is a model for rational-emotive therapists to pursue (see e.g., Ellis, 1974; Ellis & Harper, 1978). Although Ellis is undoubtedly a therapist *extraordinaire,* a clinician considering the merits of the confrontational approach might benefit by knowing that several aspects of Ellis's demeanor "stack the deck" in his therapeutic favor. These aspects are relevant to the present chapter and bear further discussion.

To observe Ellis in vivo, for example, is to appreciate an extremely quick wit, a propensity for logical argument, and an unmistakable air of authority. Attesting to these qualities are hundreds of books and articles, an international reputation, a professional training institute (the Institute for Rational Living) and a substantial professional following. As the social psychological literature has shown, the aura of expertise lays fertile ground for attitude change (e.g., Aronson, 1972). Hence, a famous therapist has a persuasive advantage with many clients even before their therapy begins.

What do therapists do when the scales of recognition are not so heavily tipped in their favor? We have had the opportunity to exchange ideas with many excellent clinicians who practice or who have tried to practice RET via the confrontational approach. A seemingly invariable problem is the client's reaction once his or her ideas have been given such labels as "irrational," "crazy," "mistaken," or "neurotic." In the confrontational approach clients tend to perceive that they as well as their ideas are being attacked, and anger, depression, missed sessions, and treatment dropouts often ensue.

One possible solution to this problem is a plush office, a name plaque advertising an advanced degree, and blatantly observable diplomas and professional awards. An overpowering air of authority can also be of service.

Although other solutions are limited only to one's imagination (see Haley, 1973), the solution proposed here is quite different from attempting to employ a confrontational approach more effectively. The therapist neither decides which of the client's beliefs are rational or irrational nor supplies the arguments to support such judgments. Instead, this procedure is performed *by the client,* so that the elements of interpersonal confrontation are removed. As with other CRT techniques, this process is accomplished by a series of graduated directives that progress from an objective to a personal point of view.

FEELINGS ARE NOT NECESSARILY TRUE

The first step in this progression involves convincing the client that what he or she feels is true is not necessarily true. Beck (1976) expresses this as the difference between fact and opinion. We ask the client to state something that was believed by ancient cultures but that is no longer considered true. Common answers are that the world was flat, that gods controlled the weather, that all planets moved around the earth, and that illness was caused by bad blood or evil spirits.

Next, the client is asked to remember a superstition, myth, or fairy tale that he or she believed as a child but no longer believes as an adult. Such childhood beliefs as Santa Claus and the Easter Bunny are commonly stated. We point out that such beliefs, although strongly held at one time, turned out to be false, and we ask, "Do you see that it is possible for someone to feel strongly about something that isn't true?"

BELIEFS CAN BE CHANGED

Even though clients almost always answer in the affirmative, they often think, "So what? If you believe in something, there's nothing you can really do about it." We counter this implicit assumption by asking clients why they no longer believe in Santa Claus (or whatever myth they have stated). They usually say, "Because I read something that changed my mind," "Because other people told me it wasn't so," or "Because I really stopped to think about it." We concur with these observations and add that beliefs are changed constantly by reading, experience, and the like. For example, "What if you heard on the news that it was going to be 60 degrees the next day and walked outside in your tennis shorts to find it snowing? You would change your belief in that weather prediction pretty fast, wouldn't you?"

We explain that feelings are learned through experiences that influence us to think in certain ways. And we point out, the number of times we repeat or model these thoughts largely determines how strongly subsequent emotions are experienced. This argument puts the client in a dilemma which we express as, "If feelings and thoughts are not necessarily based on objective reality, then how does one determine if they are really true?"

ANALYZING THE Bs

We introduce analysis to our clients by drawing a picture of a cat and a camera (Fig. 8–1). The cat represents the situation (A), the image of the cat in the camera represents the consequence (C), and the lens of the camera represents the belief (B). We draw the client inside the camera and say, "Imagine that you look through the lens and see a red cat. How can you find out whether or not the cat is truly red? The lens, after all, may have a filter over it. Such a filter would be like a false belief that inaccurately colors our perceptions of events. How could you tell if the cat is really red?"

With our coaching, clients come up with several solutions, such as ask people on the outside about the cat, ask a lens expert or a cat expert, or see if the cat's color ever changes. We say, "When we want to gather evidence that something is really true, we can critically examine our own experience, ask other people, consult an expert, and so on. I want to show you a method for determining whether or not your Bs are true. You can use this to see for yourself if what you feel is based on fact or on fallacy. Okay?"

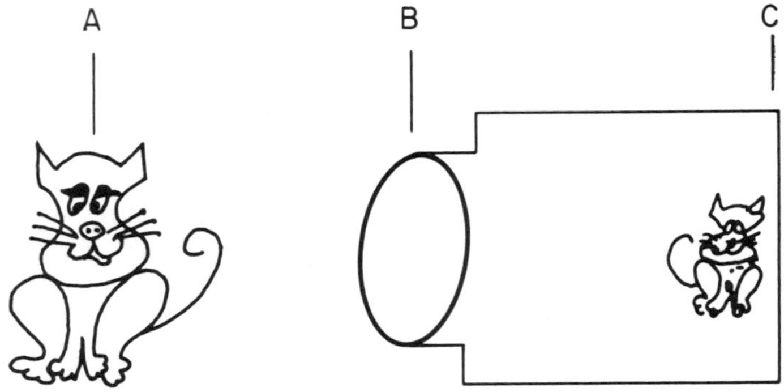

Fig. 8–1. Cat–camera analogy.

Attention is now shifted to an examination of the client's own beliefs. This process is systematically directed and has several therapeutic advantages that will be listed and discussed near the end of this chapter.

Client's Judgment of the Bs

Most of our clients have approximately 30 beliefs on their master list by the time that analysis is addressed (usually at the fourth CRT session). These include the core beliefs and their related surface beliefs. We begin the work of analysis by asking clients to judge the beliefs on their lists as true or false. Typically clients will judge the majority of these Bs as false by use of the following technique. They imagine themselves as objective, rational scientists who are to decide whether each B on the master list is true or false according to logical criteria. (The choice of criteria is left to the client.) If clients feel that a belief is true but "know" that it is not, they are to put an F (for false) beside it on the list. The "objective" truth or falsity of a belief takes precedence over its affective quality.

The therapist does not argue with any verdict at this point. If the client says, "I objectively rule that I am truly the lowliest nerd that ever lived," the therapist says, "Okay. That one is true for you. How about the next one?" Clients often have a remarkable talent for objective analysis, and a verdict of false to every belief on the list is not uncommon. If this occurs, the analysis is complete, and the material on *countering* (see Chapter 9) is promptly addressed. Usually, however, from two to seven of the beliefs on the master list remain true. If the therapist thinks that these remaining Bs are not crucial to treatment, the analysis is complete, and preparation for countering is begun. If one or more of these Bs is crucial, however, we go on to the *checklist analysis*. For example, one client, who isolated himself from women because of sexual performance anxiety, produced a self-rated master list in which three statements rated "true" were considered crucial (see Table 8–1). This client felt that every one of his beliefs was true, but objectively rated all except three of them as false. These three merited further examination, and the second step in the analysis was addressed.

Checklist Analysis

In the second step, the client is presented with a checklist of five questions (see also Appendix B), adapted from Maultsby (1971) by author McMullin. Each question must be answered "yes" or "no" and is directed to one B at a time.

1. Does the belief make me feel better?
2. Does the belief help me accomplish my goals?
3. Does the belief help me get along better with others?
4. Would everybody have the same belief in this situation?
5. Do I always feel this way in similar situations?

This exercise dramatically proves to clients the uselessness of their irrational beliefs. Clients will answer "no" to most questions about their irrational beliefs. Furthermore, they will rate many beliefs false as a result of the checklist procedure.

One drawback of the checklist is its logical inconsistency (e.g., beliefs that do not accomplish goals and that do not improve relationships with others are usually but not automatically false). The client may say, "I don't see how something that makes me feel bad is necessarily false. For example, I know that I'm going to die someday. This belief makes me feel bad, yet it's very true." Hence the checklist procedure cannot be used to judge a belief true or false. If a client is not completely convinced that his or her Bs are false based on the checklist or if several Bs remain on the list, we then switch to linguistic analysis.

It is should be evident from this discussion that we place great importance on the verdict of true or false. (We prefer the term "false" to such terms as "irrational," "crazy," or "neurotic.") Several years ago, author McMullin skipped this step as an experiment and went directly to the voluntary cortical inhibition and the self-punishment–self-reward techniques (see Chapters 10 and 11). The outcome was initially unsuccessful in over 50 percent of the cases because clients consistently stated, "How can I realistically argue against something I know to be true?" This problem is never encountered when clients first decide for themselves that a belief lacks objective validity.

Table 8–1
Self-Rated Master List

Belief	Rating*
If I don't have a spontaneous erection when I make love I am totally worthless.	F
If I don't have a spontaneous erection, my partner will automatically have contempt for me.	F
It would be awful if my partner had contempt for me.	T†
If my partner had contempt for me I would be totally worthless.	T†
I have to have sex to live.	T†
I have to have a large penis to perform adequately.	F
If I don't have a spontaneous erection I'm less than a man.	F
True men never have problems like this.	F
Being less than a man is awful.	F
If I'm less than a man I'm worthless.	F
It's disgraceful to have this problem.	F
It's all society's fault that I have hang-ups about sex.	F
It's all my parents' fault that I have hang-ups about sex.	F
I shouldn't have to work on this problem; it isn't fair.	F

*T = true, F = false.
†Ratings of "true" made these beliefs crucial.

To review, the following steps are taken before linguistic analysis is addressed:

1. We ask the client to state a past cultural belief that has been proven false.
2. We ask the client to state a personal belief that has been proven false.
3. We draw and explain the cat and camera analogy.
4. We have the client objectively judge all Bs on the master list as true or false.
5. If all Bs are false or if the "true" Bs are inconsequential, we proceed to the countering section.
6. If one or more therapeutically crucial Bs remain, we present the checklist.
7. If any significant Bs still are present, we introduce linguistic analysis.

Linguistic Analysis

The clinician who has progressed to Step 7 above, is faced with one or more Bs that the client believes to be true and that must be proven false for cognitive treatment efficacy to be maximized. This problem calls for linguistic analysis, a modification of a procedure explained by Wilson (1956).

According to Wilson (1956, p. 76), in order to determine that any belief or statement is true, we must have three things:

1. Knowledge of the statement's meaning
2. Knowledge of the right way to verify it
3. Good evidence for believing it

For simplicity we translate the foregoing into the three steps of (1) defining your terms, (2) deciding your rules, and (3) finding your evidence.

It is important to note that core Bs, although sometimes expressed in isolation while we are in the phase of finding specific cognitions (e.g., "I'm worthless "), are always connected to events during the analysis and treatment phases (e.g., "I should feel worthless because my supervisor misses our meetings"). We explain this to the client in the context of the analysis:

> Of course, it is certainly true that you feel worthless in a number of different situations. But that isn't the issue, is it? We want to decide whether or not you *have* to feel this way or whether you have simply learned to feel this way.

DEFINING TERMS

We define the major words in the client's stated belief by progressively decreasing levels of abstraction. We may use a dictionary if necessary. This step is crucial because nearly all Bs are rated false once their terms are properly specified. We illustrate this process for the reader with the following verbatim example:

> **Therapist:** As best you could objectively determine, some of your Bs are true, and others are false. One of the interesting qualities of beliefs is that they can go by us so quickly and at such high levels of abstraction that they are hard to evaluate objectively.
>
> Take this table, for example: this *table* is a low level of abstraction. If we wanted to go to higher levels, we might progress from *table* to *furniture,* to *wood,* and then to *thing* or *object. Thing* and *wood* describe a lot of stuff in this room, but this *table* describes only one thing. I could point to it and say "kitchen sink," and you could immediately disagree because we would be working at a low enough level of abstraction.
>
> This is what I want to teach you to do with the rest of your Bs. We have written them at such a high abstraction level that it's hard for you to tell whether or not they're really true. I want to teach you how to slow your beliefs down and examine them specifically so that you can judge them true or false more accurately.
>
> Let's start with one of your own beliefs. As written in a fairly abstract form it reads like this: "I believe I should feel worthless because I don't perform perfectly in college."
>
> **Client:** Yeah.
>
> **T:** Okay, let's begin by defining the major terms. The major terms are *should, worthless,* and *perform perfectly*. The dictionary says that *should* means "to have an obligation to." That's a high level of abstraction. To whom or what are you obliged to feel rotten?
>
> **C:** Well, to my parents, now that I think about it. They used to be very disappointed when I didn't make straight As.
>
> **T:** Okay, that's specific enough. What does *worthless* mean to you?
>
> **C:** Just what it says. Totally without worth—without any redeeming qualities.

T: And *perform perfectly?*

C: Well, that means to make better grades than everyone else.

T: All right, now I'm going to rewrite this sentence, and then we can decide what evidence would prove it true or false: "Because my parents would be disappointed, I am totally without worth and have no redeeming qualities whatsoever if I don't make better grades than every other student at my school."

C: God, that's screwy. Definitely false.

T: How come?

C: Well, what my parents feel is *their* problem. Besides, I have worthy qualities regardless of my test scores. Why should I be so concerned with those other clowns at school, anyway?

T: Okay. Fine. You now know that it's false, but you still *feel* that it's true. Right?

C: Yes. As silly as it is. I still feel it.

T: That is what the rest of the therapy is about.

DECIDING RULES AND FINDING EVIDENCE

Sometimes clients are still not sure whether the specific form of a belief is false. In these cases, we ask for evidence that would prove it true or false, and then we examine this evidence:

T: Your belief as written in a fairly abstract form reads like this: "I ought to feel like I'm less than a man if I don't have a spontaneous erection when making love."

C: That's it.

T: Okay, let's define the major terms in this sentence. The major terms are *ought to, less than a man,* and *spontaneous erection.* The dictionary defines *ought* as "having an obligation to." To whom or what are you obliged to feel miserable?

C: Well, when I was in high school, I ran around with some macho types who were always saying that kind of stuff.

T: And you began saying, it, too?

C: I sure did.

T: All right, that's specific enough. And what does *less than a man* mean to you?

C: God, I don't know. Let me see—I guess it means completely incapable of being a decent lover—incapable of satisfying a woman sexually.

T: And *spontaneous erection?*

C: I was always told that a real man has an erection within a second after foreplay begins.
T: Okay. Let's write this sentence out completely and then look for evidence: "Because my high school buddies said so, I am completely incapable of satisfying a woman sexually when I don't have spontaneous erections within one second after foreplay begins."
C: That seems kind of stupid, doesn't it?
T: Well, I don't know. What kind of evidence would we need to prove that belief true or false?
C: It would be true if all adequate lovers had erections within one second of foreplay.
T: Good. Would you agree that it would also be true if everything your buddies said about sex was correct?
C: Yes. And it would be false if we could find exceptions.
T: Right. Remember the cat and camera example? You can find out the color of the cat by using your own experience, asking others, or asking an expert. Which of these would be appropriate in your case?
C: Oh—I could use my experience. I could find out if I could satisfy a woman without a spontaneous erection.
T: Good. Anything else?
C: Yeah. I could ask an expert. You're an expert on this stuff. What do you think?
T: I think that your belief is false, but I would like you to have a second opinion. Would you be willing to read parts of *The Hite Report* or Zilbergeld's *Male Sexuality* this week?
C: Sure.
T: Okay. I will tell you the most relevant chapters, and we will discuss them next week.

The foregoing cases have been presented for purposes of clarification. Clinicians who first attempt this technique are advised that all analyses do not go as simply or as quickly as these and that many clients require more coaching.

We have never had a client rate a crucial belief as true once it has been examined by the linguistic analysis technique. Should such an event occur—and we are sure that it is possible—the therapist has at least one option: work on removing the antecedent event. Suppose, for example, that a client rates the following belief as true: "Because my parents said so,

I am totally devoid of any redeeming qualities if I don't know the exact definition of all of my husband's big words." In this instance, we would either increase the client's vocabulary or teach the husband to alter his conversation. If neither of these procedures is workable, the client should be told that the probability of success with CRT is reduced. (A belief rated as true tends to override cognitive interventions designed to challenge its validity.) Other treatment options can then be explored.

SUMMARY

Teaching the client logical analysis has the following therapeutic advantages:

1. It avoids resistance as an outgrowth of the confrontational approach.
2. It allows clients to decide for themselves whether or not a belief is true.
3. It gives the client a method of analysis which can be used independently of the therapist once treatment is completed. This contributes to maintenance of therapeutic gains and more skillful handling of other problems that may arise.
4. It encourages the client to think critically and objectively.
5. It helps develop counters to the master list beliefs.

The homework for the week is as follows:

- The client is asked to continue analyzing any remaining "true" Bs not addressed in the session.
- The logical analysis section of *Talk Sense to Yourself* is also assigned.

In order to encourage clients at the end of this session (some need it), we congratulate them on their demonstrated perseverence in therapy and explain that the next session will involve direct countering of their Bs in order to begin reducing negative emotions.

PART IV

Therapeutic Interventions

In this section, several techniques are presented that are designed to alter the client's maladaptive cognitive patterns. The therapeutic negation of these patterns by means of cognitive procedures represents the final stage of treatment and the most important direct contribution to emotional relief.

9

Principles of Countering

The material on countering is usually presented at the sixth cognitive restructuring therapy session and represents the first attempt at direct therapeutic intervention. Even this session, however, is biased towards preparation for later techniques; therefore, clients are not expected to reap immediate or significant benefits from the material in this chapter alone.

HIERARCHY CONSTRUCTION

The first phase of preparation involves *hierarchy construction,* adapted from Wolpe (1969, 1973), to include verbal as well as imaginal aspects of emotional distress. It is through hierarchy construction that the therapeutic contract is further negotiated and defined. Clients often have more than one affective or behavioral complaint that would benefit from therapeutic attention, and it is their option to decide which of these is most immediately in need of change. We address one or two such complaints but emphasize while doing so that the clients may apply the same procedures to other complaints. Clients who learn this methodology become their own counselors capable of handling remaining or upcoming problems by themselves.

We use two primary methods of hierarchy construction, types A and B.

Type A

Type A construction is used when an emotion is maintained primarily by four or more beliefs. The therapist begins by teaching the client to discriminate *subjective units of disturbance,* abbreviated as SUDs. (The term subjective unit of disturbance [S.U.D.] is adapted from Wolpe, 1973, p. 120.) We ask the client to close his or her eyes and briefly imagine the worst A–B–C situation involving the target emotion that he or she has ever experienced. The intensity of that emotion is assigned 10 SUDs, on a scale of 1–10. The client then imagines an A–B–C event in which the target emotion was just barely perceived. This intensity is rated as 1 SUD. Finally, the client chooses a situation that would be rated as 5 SUDs. As the client is imagining these events, the therapist writes down the specific As and Bs on a hierarchy sheet (see Appendix C). We get a brief description of sights, sounds, smells, and other details of the As and, then we list the specific cognitions involved in each of these situations. (This information greatly facilitates the *voluntary cortical inhibition* and *self-punishment–self-reward* techniques addressed in later sessions.)

When clients even briefly imagine the 10-SUD event, they tend to become upset. For this reason, we always start with the 10 and progress from it to the other events (instead of vice versa). This tends to relieve or ameliorate the client's distress. The client is asked to fill in the hierarchy sheet at home with seven other A–B–C events (one for each SUD level). The numerous A–B–C in the client's notebook are available in this regard.

Three other facts of note should be mentioned about this method:

1. Only the emotional intensity of the situations are ranked on the hierarchy, not the Bs. Thus clients will list only 10 situations, but they may have 20 or 30 Bs connected to these As.
2. Biofeedback can be a useful supplement to hierarchy construction, and it is especially impressive to those interested in scientific instrumentation. We find it appropriate for use (i.e., the biofeedback reading correlates with subjective impressions) with one client in seven.
3. CRT hierarchy construction relies more on memory of past traumas than on the ability to experience them through imagery in the session. For this reason, it is a viable approach even with the 10 to 15 percent of clients who are not facile with imagery (Wolpe, 1969).

Here is an example of a "guilt" hierarchy (McMullin & Casey, 1975, p. 40):

1. Not cleaning room
2. Spending too much money

3. Watching too much television
4. Not going to church
5. Not getting a job
6. Not spending "enough" time with kids
7. Not calling mother "enough"
8. Never having finished school
9. Staying out late with men
10. Getting involved in a past affair

Type B

Type B hierarchy construction is used when an emotion is maintained by three or fewer beliefs. (This situation is somewhat more unusual than that calling for the Type A method.) In this case, we mount a more concentrated attack on the core beliefs by isolating them into situation–response (A–C) categories that clearly exemplify a particular maladaptive thought pattern. If clients have two or three core thoughts, they first rank each thought in terms of "believability" (least, moderately, or most believable). For example, one of our clients had three thoughts which caused all his anxiety and depression—"I am crazy," "I am sinful," and "I am inferior "—but he believed each thought to different degrees. He only weakly and occasionally thought he was crazy, but he strongly and frequently felt inferior. By ranking these core thoughts, we could attack his weakest thought first.

After the cores are ranked, the client relates in the manner previously described, three A–C events (eliciting low, medium, and high SUD levels) for each thought (see Appendix D for the corresponding hierarchy form) With Type B we do not request seven additional A–C situations to supplement the low-, medium-, and high-SUD items.

An example of a Type B hierarchy is presented in Table 9–1. (The cognitions associated with the As are not listed.) The client in question wanted to eliminate her feelings of self-worthlessness. The therapist would need to get a better description of the A–C examples presented in the table before advanced countering techniques could be properly applied. This procedure is further elaborated in the next chapter.

COUNTERING

After hierarchy construction has been addressed, the topic is switched to *countering*. A *counter* is defined as a thought that argues against another thought and includes such activities as thinking or behaving in an opposite

Table 9–1
Type B Hierarchy of Client with Feelings of Self-Worthlessness

Core Belief	Believability	Situation–Response (A–C)	
		Description	SUDs*
		The presidential candidate the client supported did not win.	1
"What other people think makes it so."	Least Believable	A friend expressed distate for a novel the client really enjoyed.	4
		The client spilled a drink on a customer at work. The customer called her a "stupid, bumbling fool."	7
		The client feels slightly tense every morning.	2
"I'm sick."	Moderately Believable	She got angry at her boyfriend and threw a book at him.	6
		She felt like staying in bed (and did so) for three days.	8
		The client's boyfriend beat her in a game of chess.	3
"I'm worthless."	Most Believable	The client was turned down at a job interview.	6
		Because she made a driving error, she caused a car accident.	9

*SUDs = subjective units of disturbance

direction, arguing in a very assertive fashion, and convincing oneself of the falsity of a belief. Clients are asked to write this definition in their notebooks.

We next will model the countering technique with examples that progressively approximate those appropriate to the client's problem. A segment of such a dialogue might proceed as follows:

> Now watch me, and I'll show you a few counters. Let's say that all my life I believed that everyone just had to love me. This included my boss, my teachers, my dates, the milkman, and others. Now let's say I decide that this belief is false and that I want to change it so as to become less ingratiating and subservient to other people. I would begin by saying to myself things like this: "What would really be so horrible about being disliked by somebody? The world wouldn't blow up, now would it? And I wouldn't be such a crum, either. This damned belief is making me too scared to enjoy myself around people. What bullshit! I don't have to buy this!" Do you see what I mean?

We explain the rules for countering to clients and have them write them in their notebooks. The rules for effective counters are as follows:

1. *Counters must be directly opposite to the false belief.* For example, if the irrational belief was, "I'm worthless if I make a bad grade," a directly opposite counter would be, "My grade on this test has nothing to do with my worth as a person," not "It would be lousy if I failed this test, but I can stand it."
2. *Counters must be believable statements of reality.* For example, "I don't need everyone to love me to be happy," is a reasonable statement; "It doesn't matter at all if nobody likes me" is not.
3. *The client should develop as many counters as possible.* We draw a scale for the client at this point that is tipped in favor of the core beliefs. We explain that the core beliefs have much weight because of the number of repetitions they have endured over time. Thus, to tip the balance in the client's favor, many strong counters are needed that will override the accumulated effects of the cores.
4. *Counters must be created by the client (with coaching from the therapist only if necessary).* Counters that would be

effective for the therapist are not always effective for the client. Furthermore, it has been our experience that clients are more likely to argue against counters that are not of their own making.

5. *Counters must be concise.* The most frequent countering mistake made at first is using "dissertations." Counters should be easy to remember so that they can be used with little hesitation or delay.
6. *Counters must be stated with assertive, aggressive, and/or emotional intensity.*

Many clients begin countering in an automatic, mechanical, and unconvincing way. We have them repeat a counter nasally, then mechanically (i.e., without feeling), and then with vigor, filling their lungs with air and vehemently stating the new belief. The latter style of countering is what we are trying to produce.

Using these rules, the client is asked to provide counters for several of the 45 Bs listed in Appendix A. This gives the client an opportunity to practice and to receive feedback from the therapist. The beliefs from the client's own master list are next addressed in this fashion until counters for each are available (given that time permits). The therapist helps with this process by asking questions such as, "Which phrases can you use to convince yourself that this belief isn't true?" and "What experiences prove that it isn't true?" The linguistic analysis technique greatly facilitates this process by giving the client experience in determining the false components of his or her beliefs. All viable counters are written by the client in his or her notebook.

Homework following this session is as follows:

- Fill in remaining hierarchy items and three or four corresponding Bs (Type A only).
- Write counters for any master-list Bs not addressed in the session.

Clients are also told to practice some of the counters at home if they want to, but not to expect to feel much better as a result. For reasons delineated in the next chapter, initial success is not likely to occur until more systematic countering procedures (in conjunction with the hierarchies) are utilized.

10
Voluntary Cortical Inhibition

Consistent with a neobehaviorist approach, the *voluntary cortical inhibition* (VCI) procedure is designed to influence perceptions, cognitions, and beliefs that contribute to negative affect (McMullin & Casey, 1975). The development of VCI was largely influenced by Wolpe's work (e.g., 1958, 1973). Positive affect elicited by rational cognitions was believed to reciprocally inhibit the painful autonomic responses that were the targets of intervention. Recently, several alternative hypotheses have been made to explain the effects of systematic desensitization, and the reciprocal inhibition hypothesis has been strongly criticized (e.g., Kazdin & Wilcoxin, 1976; Meichenbaum, 1977). We prefer not to take sides in this debate, because its resolution lies with future empirical results, not preliminary opinion. Thus, in the meantime, we are receptive to the possibility that our therapeutic success might be due to such factors as efficacy expectations (Bandura, 1977b), exposure (Marks, 1978), expectancy (Kazdin & Wilcoxin, 1976), counterconditioning (Bandura, 1969), or coping skills (Meichenbaum, 1977). We also feel that the reciprocal inhibition hypothesis is still a viable possibility. Wolpe (1981) has noted that the experimental evidence against reciprocal inhibition has been marked by methodological flaws such as analogue subject populations, poorly trained therapists, inadequate relaxation training, and so on. These flaws must be addressed before firm conclusions can be drawn.

In the meantime, we contend that feelings are to a large degree conditioned by learning experiences. Since most clients have had years of conditioning of their thoughts, feelings, and behavior, subsequent relief usually requires hard and extended effort above and beyond the point of philosophical inquiry. When clients are made to understand this point, they become less likely to punish themselves for feeling miserable despite insight into the logical fallacies of their complaints.

Most of the cognitive therapies attack irrational cognitions with negligible systematic regard for general cognitive "believability," breadth of cognitive influence, or strength of engendered affect. This can lead the client to inflated expectations of the power of therapeutic self-statements, thereby biasing him or her toward discouragement with the countering technique (e.g., "Damn! I told myself it wouldn't be awful if she rejected me, but that didn't make me feel any better. This stuff must not be working"). In addition to our theoretical notions, it has been our practical experience that countering procedures work best when systematically directed to the easiest A–C events first. This allows greater opportunity for the client to achieve immediate success and subsequent feelings of self-efficacy.

INTRODUCTION TO THE SESSION

In addition to the usual procedures followed at the beginning of a session, we introduce the VCI session with a checklist of questions that assess whether or not the client is actually ready for this technique. These questions proceed as follows:

- Do you agree that your problems are mainly caused by your beliefs (as opposed to your wife, your repressed libido, etc.)?
- Do you think that we have gotten the specific Bs that are causing the problems? Have we missed any?
- What are your core beliefs?
- Do you know that they are false?
- Do you know how to analyze your beliefs so that you can deem them true or false in the future?

Clients usually answer all the foregoing questions in the affirmative. Any disagreements or hedges at this point can be extremely helpful because they predict resistances or doubts that, if not immediately addressed, will obstruct therapeutic progress in the long run. One client, for example, expressed a fear of being helpless if she could no longer blame her husband for her distress. This fear prompted further cognitive and behavioral exploration so that assertive (versus helpless or aggressive) responses were substituted for angry ones.

Once the checklist exercise is complete, the client is told why the rational way of thinking will at first be uncomfortable and hard to master. The first analogy we use in this regard is borrowed from Maultsby (1974).

> **Therapist:** You may wonder why you still *feel* that your master-list Bs are true and why the counters seem a bit unnatural. I compare this with driving in England. If you were there for the first time, driving on the left side of the road would feel very uncomfortable. You would *know* that the left side is correct, but you wouldn't feel comfortable with it. This is like your old way of thinking versus the new way. The new way will not seem at all comfortable to you at first even though you know it is right. How would you eventually learn to feel comfortable driving on the left side of the road?
>
> **Client:** I guess by continuing to do it.
>
> **T:** Right! And that is what people seldom do when they try to change their thinking. They don't know that continued, daily practice over and over is needed before a new attitude can *feel* true as well as *be* true.

We supplement this analogy with one concerning the acquisition of a foreign language:

> **T:** This is also similar to learning another language. You certainly wouldn't expect to learn it in a week, and the memorization and pronunciation of the foreign words would be quite difficult at first. However, if you practiced daily, you would eventually feel much more skilled and comfortable with these words. Rational thinking is a lot like a foreign language. It will take much practice before it feels natural to you, and progress will occur gradually over time.

We may add to the above with further analogies (such as learning a musical instrument) or with counterconditioning explanations of cognitive change for clients who would be interested. In addition to making the VCI presentation clearer, such analogies stress the importance of practice, and they reduce any expectations of immediate, sudden, or drastic change. We explain to clients that, at first, they will probably revert to their old ways of thinking in times of stress (just as people from other countries often revert to their native tongue when excited). Finally, we caution that therapeutic progress will entail a series of ups and downs and that counters work better on some days than on others. All of the above are preventive measures that encourage the client to practice and to persevere in spite of the inevitable difficulties that will ensue. If such measures are not taken, the client, upon encountering continued problems, becomes more likely to attribute failure to the therapy, the therapist, or to himself or herself.

VOLUNTARY CORTICAL INHIBITION

Voluntary cortical inhibition itself is introduced with an explanation of its terms. Eysenck (1957) has conceptualized certain psychological problems as due to a failure to inhibit certain thoughts. With VCI, such thoughts are inhibited voluntarily; hence, "voluntary" cortical inhibition. The hierarchy items and counters are checked for specificity of detail, and the therapist keeps these at hand while guiding VCI. As with most cognitive restructuring therapy techniques, the steps to VCI are explained in advance so that the client will know what to expect:

> **T:** I will pick the item lowest on your hierarchy and describe it for you. You will relax, close your eyes, and try to imagine this scene as vividly as you possibly can. When you get a vivid image, you will raise your right index finger. I will then ask you to think the Bs exactly as you think them in the situation. You will probably feel the emotion you usually feel, but you are not required to feel it very intensely. When you have both the A and Bs clearly in mind, raise your finger. I will say "Stop," and you will begin thinking the counters in place of the old Bs. I will let you do this for about a minute, and then we will try it two more times. Okay?

The item assigned the lowest subjective-unit-of-disturbance rating is then addressed, and the client is asked to imagine the A and the Bs and to report the subsequent SUD level. (This baseline reading is usually between 2 and 4 SUDs. If it is any higher, we substitute a less threatening image until the SUDs decrease to the appropriate level.) The full procedure is then instigated for three repetitions, one of which is illustrated verbatim below:

> **T:** I want you to close your eyes and relax. That's it. Just relax all over—let your whole body go loose and limp. Let yourself get heavy. This is your time to relax. [pause] Now imagine that

> your boss is looking over one of your reports. See his face. Be aware of any sights, sounds, and smells in the room. See all the colors and all the details. Think only about this scene. When you get that image clearly in mind, raise your finger—okay. Now begin thinking the Bs you usually have in this situation. When you get the image and the thoughts clearly in mind, raise your finger—stop! Now begin arguing against those thoughts as hard as you can. Work hard! Convince yourself that they are irrational and destructive. Attack them and challenge them in every way that you can. Do this for about a minute and concentrate 100 percent. [one minute pause] When those counters are clearly in mind, raise your finger.

The foregoing repetition is presented two more times with minor variations:

- The A and the Bs are presented together.
- Instructions become shorter and more concise.
- The "Stop" intervention follows between 1 and 7 seconds after the finger raise so that the irrational thoughts (versus the finger raise itself) predict this signal.

Although clear visualization facilitates this technique, it is not essential. When clients have visualization problems, we ask them to get as much of the image as they can and concentrate more on thinking the corresponding Bs. We do not demand or suggest that any client acutely feel the emotion involved for this might cause further sensitization to the situation.

Once the three repetitions are complete, we ask the client to imagine the A and the Bs *without the counters* in order to get another SUD reading. About 70 percent of clients treated in group sessions (see Chapter 14) will have a drop of between 1 and 2 SUDs from baseline. No change will be seen in 20 percent, and SUDs will increase in 10 percent. Among clients seen individually, only 10 percent will fail to experience diminished discomfort. When such failures occur we quickly and confidently state that the SUDs failed to drop for one or more of the following reasons:

- The counters were repeated mechanically and without vehement attack.
- The client added imaginal or verbal elements to the scene that increased its potency.
- The client argued against the counters.
- The countering was too indirect.
- The client countered the wrong Bs.

We assess which of the foregoing reasons caused the problem, give the client feedback, and proceed to the next set of repetitions (which every client performs). *Counter control* will also cause VCI failure and is discussed in Chapter 12.

The next set of repetitions is begun by having the client describe out loud the exact images, beliefs, and counters that were employed in the first VCI trials. This step allows the therapist to further inspect and improve the efficacy of this procedure. Many clients, for example, will not be countering in an aggressive fashion, and the therapist can model the way this is to be done and ask the client to follow suit. When the client has overtly demonstrated VCI satisfactorily, an A–B SUD reading is taken and two more covert VCI trials are completed in the manner described above.

A final A–B SUD reading is taken before the homework is assigned. Only one client in a hundred will fail to decrease his subjective discomfort by this point, and such a failure is almost always attributable to a "control" issue of some kind (see Chapter 13). The majority of clients will also report feeling tired at this point owing to the concentration involved with the VCI technique.

The homework for the week is as follows:

> The client is asked to spend 20–30 minutes per day in quiet, uninterrupted, and preferably scheduled VCI practice. The client works on the lowest hierarchy item until the SUD level is reduced to 0 or 1. The next highest item is then addressed until it, too, is reduced to 1 SUD or below. For a Type A hierarchy, this procedure may be continued until even the highest-SUD item no longer elicits distress. (Usually, clients get only to the second or third item the first week.) For a Type B hierarchy, the items under the least believable core are progressively addressed until diminished to 1 SUD or below. The next most believable core may then be addressed (and so on) until the problem is relieved.

In order to help prevent perceived failure with the homework, we carefully address the following pitfalls so as to reduce inflated expectations of success:

1. An item that has been reduced to SUD level of 0 or 1 should be practiced two days subsequently to overlearn the effect.
2. If a client becomes particularly distressed over one of the A–C situations, he or she is to drop it completely and go to another one. The painful item can be dealt with at the next session.

3. VCI is approximately 50 percent as powerful when done alone as when the therapist assists.
4. If clients become confused about some aspect of the VCI procedure, they are to call the therapist as soon as possible.
5. The effectiveness of the counters will vary slightly from one day to another. Hence, a hierarchy item that is easily reduced one day may be more difficult the next.
6. The SUD level of an imagined situation will climb if the situation is encountered in vivo. (If clients expect this, they will not be so readily discouraged.) We recommend that the client avoid painful A–C situations this week whenever possible.
7. Usually, about 50 to 90 repetitions of VCI are required to significantly reduce all of the original SUD ratings (see Figure 10–1).

We sometimes use biofeedback procedures with our clients. With approximately one client in seven, biofeedback on heart-rate output correlates with SUDs and discriminates imagined negative situations from neutral ones. With VCI, pulse rates tend to increase when painful A–C situations are imagined (the higher the item, the faster the pulse) and should increase at least 10 beats per minute over the resting rate to be clinically useful. When countering is done correctly, the pulse rate increases at first (due to the effort required) and then decreases below baseline levels. The client who is making some mistake with the counters, can be corrected very quickly with this technique, because the heart rate will not decline appropriately.

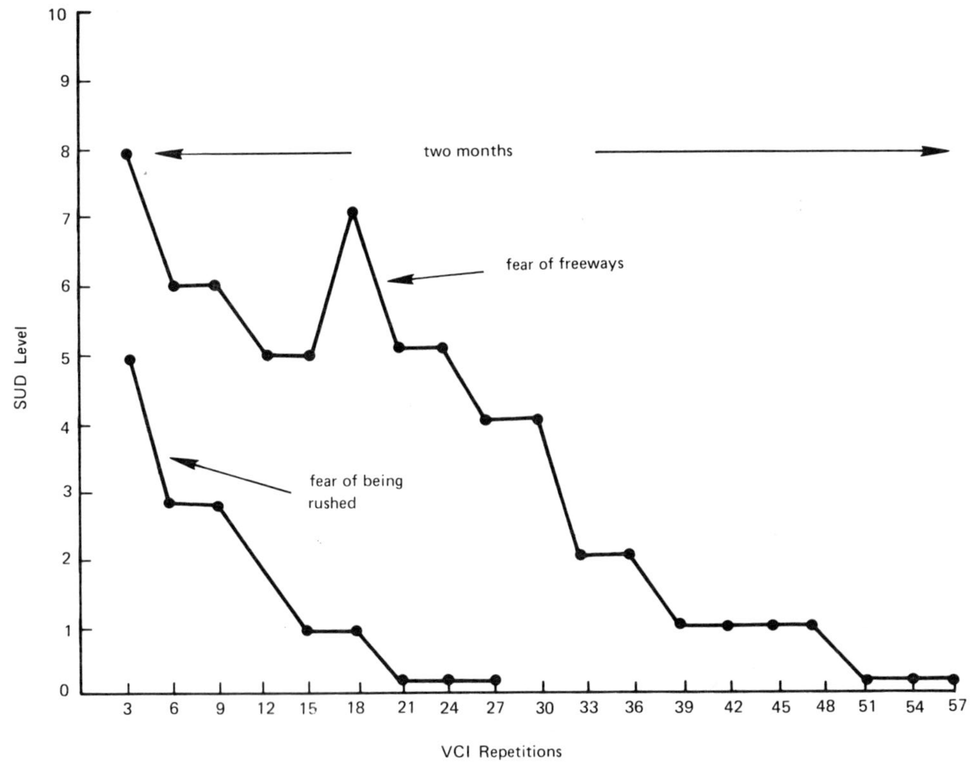

Fig. 10–1. Reduction of two phobias in a 32-year-old client using voluntary cortical inhibition.

11

Self-Punishment–Self-Reward

Clients will rarely return from the first week of voluntary cortical inhibition homework with the SUD levels of all their hierarchy items reduced to 0 and with little need to continue treatment. Most still have many problems. We review their homework, assess any difficulties they are having with the VCI technique and give further practice when necessary. If the SUDs have dropped to criterion on two or more of the hierarchy items (the probability of this happening is about 70 percent) and if we are sure that the VCI has been sufficiently mastered, the *self-punishment–self-reward* (SP–SR) technique is introduced. The technique of punishing inappropriate thoughts while rewarding realistic beliefs has several therapeutic advantages:

- It adds novelty to the intervention, thereby reducing satiation or boredom with VCI.
- It addresses rewarding and punishing images instead of the more verbal techniques or VCI.
- It helps reduce operant payoffs for the presented symptomatology by focusing on the disadvantages of irrational thinking and on the substitution of a more reinforcing response.

PREPARATION

SP–SR is introduced to the client as the second tool in the intervention process. The therapist picks a belief that is unrelated to the client's problems (for example, "I have to depend on others to be happy") and asks the client to punish this belief by imagining the worst possible consequences of thinking this way (e.g., "I would never do anything on my own," "I would smother other people," or "I would have low self-esteem"). Attention is then directed to the client's hierarchy item that still elicits 2 or more SUDs. We ask the client to state the worst possible consequences of *thinking* irrationally in this situation (and in others like it). It is crucial to caution the client against imagining the worst consequences of the situation rather than the thought as this might cause further sensitization to the problem. For example, the worst consequence of thinking "I must get straight As in college" may be the development of test anxiety, while the worst consequence of the situation may be flunking out of college.

Next, the client explains (with our coaching) how he or she would feel, think, and behave *ideally* in this situation and, finally, the client rewards him- or herself by imagining the best possible consequences of thinking and behaving ideally. (The therapist records all of these responses.)

It should be noted in this regard that SP–SR is used even for clients who do not produce clear imagery. We substitute cognitions for imagery when this problem occurs (i.e., "What do you *think* would be the ideal behaviors, feelings, and thoughts?"). We ensure that all imagined consequences, both positive and negative, are within realistic limits. After this preparation is complete, SP–SR is addressed. The SP–SR technique is a synthesis of Cautela's directed daydream and anxiety-relief techniques (Cautela, 1967) and further combines elements of aversive conditioning (Cautela, 1970) and covert self-reinforcement (Cautela, Walse, & Wish, 1971).

INSTRUCTION

Step 1: Following the usual relaxation instructions (see p. 72), the client is asked to imagine the A and the Bs of the target situation and to estimate the SUDs the situation elicits.

Step 2: The client imagines all the negative consequences of *thinking* these Bs in this and in all other situations. After approximately one minute of such imagery, the therapist asks the client to signal a clear image by raising his or her finger. The therapist then says, "Stop" and proceeds to Step 3.

Step 3: The client again imagines the situation and sees him- or herself thinking, feeling, and behaving in a rational manner as previously delineated. When the client signals that a clear image has been obtained, the therapist says, "Stop."

Step 4: The client imagines all the positive consequences of performing in an ideal manner in the target situation and in all other situations. The client continues this for about one minute, and then stops when a clear image has been obtained.

As in VCI, the therapist prompts most first-repetition directives by describing the target thoughts and images as derived from prior description. The process above is repeated twice more, and an A–B SUD reading is subsequently taken. This second reading is usually two points lower than the first. We assess the client's use of the technique by asking such questions as "What were the worst Cs?" "Did you get a clear image?" "What were the best Cs?" "Were they realistic?" and "Are you clear about the procedure?"

The SUDs will not drop for about 10 percent of our clientele. Together with the problems discussed in Chapter 9, the following mistakes may account for a preliminary failure with SP–SR:

- The worst consequences of the A (versus the Bs) were imagined.
- Imagery was confined to one only situation.
- The client did not imagine the best consequences of ideal performance.

If a problem has occurred on the first SP–SR set, a subsequent repetition is performed out loud, following the therapist's feedback. Once the problem is corrected (or if no problem occurred), another SP–SR set is completed silently at the therapist's direction. We continue with the same hierarchy item if it has not been reduced to one SUD or less. Otherwise, we go to the next higher A–C event on the list.

Homework following this session is as follows:

- The client is asked to do 10–15 minutes of VCI and 10–15 minutes of the SP–SR each day for the following week. Criteria for A–C mastery and advancement remain the same as in the last chapter. The client always does VCI and SP–SR on the same item in order to assess which technique works best.

- Painful A–C events are still to be avoided in vivo whenever possible. When such events are not possible to avoid, the client is told to expect some rise in subjective discomfort over that elicited through imagery alone.
- The client is asked to record the SUDs, the time spent on each exercise, and the technique used (see Appendix E). The pitfalls explained in the last chapter are reemphasized for this week.

An argument for the efficacy of *coping* imagery over *mastery* imagery has recently been made (see Meichenbaum, 1977). The SP–SR technique combines mastery and coping techniques by tempering ideal (imagined) performance with lowered expectations of success (e.g., "Don't expect to feel as anxiety-free in the real situation as you do in the imagined situation"). Coping in vivo techniques using VCI or SP–SR are presented in the next chapter.

12

In Vivo Voluntary Cortical Inhibition and Self-Punishment–Self-Reward

When the client returns from the week of voluntary cortical inhibition and self-punishment–self-reward homework, we assess, from the SUD ratings, which technique generally proved most effective. Sometimes only one of these procedures will be assigned after this assessment, although most clients find that VCI works best for certain hierarchy items and SP–SR for others.

The in vivo procedures are utilized whenever particular hierarchy items are amenable to situational exposure and have been consistently reduced to one SUD or less for 7 to 10 days. The therapist rehearses and models with the client the proper behavior and beliefs to perform when the situation is encountered and warns that the SUDs will be greater than when imagery alone is used. Since imagery is obviously unnecessary when the actual situation is encountered, certain modifications of the techniques are used for this assignment. If VCI has been the most effective technique for a particular hierarchy item, the following modifications are made:

1. Only the rational Bs (i.e., the counters) are voluntarily repeated. If the irrational Bs spontaneously occur, the client thinks, "Stop!" and continues to repeat the counters vigorously.
2. The counters are repeated until the SUDs drop one or more units from the in vivo baseline. The client is then free to leave the situation.

The modifications for the SP–SR are as follows:

1. Once the situation is encountered, the client begins to imagine all the worst possible consequences of *thinking* irrationally in the situation.
2. Once these consequences have been clearly in mind for a minute or longer, the client thinks, "Stop!" and begins to imagine the best possible consequences of behaving, thinking, and feeling rationally in the situation.
3. These steps are repeated until the SUDs drop one or more units from the in vivo baseline. The client is then free to leave the situation.

On subsequent days, the client is required to spend progressively longer periods of time performing the in vivo technique until the situation no longer is troublesome.

The therapist can tell when the treatment is working by means of several criteria:

1. The SUDs decrease. When they reach one or less, in imagination and in vivo, the therapy is terminated.
2. The A–C events become more difficult to imagine clearly.
3. The client begins to view the presented problem with an air of indifference. Statements such as "Oh, that doesn't bother me any longer" are much more common than "Thanks, Doc! You've worked miracles!" We often have to compliment clients on their therapeutic achievements; otherwise, such progress is accepted by them with striking nonchalance.
4. The counters and other components of the VIC and SP–SR come immediately to mind upon request and can be repeated without hesitation.

Subsequent homework is as follows:

- The client performs the in vivo technique five or more days on the hierarchy items that have been rated, through imagery, at one SUD or less.
- The client continues VCI or SP–SR, whichever is most effective, for the hierarchy items that still elicit significant negative affect.

Additional techniques to handle special problems are presented in the next chapter.

13

Special Problems

After introducing the reader to some general issues of control, we will discuss the following special clinical problems and the means for handling them:

- Control issues
- Sabotaging the counters
- Crisis intervention
- Denying improvement
- Working on irrelevant Bs
- Procedures with clients of low abstract intelligence
- Variants of VCI and SP–SR
- Termination

INTRODUCTION TO CLIENT CONTROL ISSUES

Perhaps the most comprehensive description and theoretical elucidation of the concepts of *resistance* and *control* in psychotherapy is given by Haley (1963). According to Haley's model, psychological symptoms occur only within an interpersonal context and arise from an unconscious attempt to control or define a relationship in self-advantageous terms. Hence, Haley views psychological symptomatology as a tool used to gain power and to set, define, and enforce rules in an interpersonal relationship.

According to Haley, the dynamics underlying control problems in a relationship also underlie resistance to therapeutic directives. If a woman develops compulsive handwashing to counter her husband's tyrannical and incessant demands, how is she to react when her therapist either says or implies, "Now cut that out!" If she consents, she not only becomes increasingly subject to her husband's domination, but she also accepts another subordinate relationship—her relationship to her therapist. The acceptance of any such relationship, according to Haley, is especially hard for "psychiatric patients" (i.e., those who seek the aid of a therapist) to accomplish; hence, control issues become manifest through the client's failure to obey directive techniques.

Although Haley presents the paradoxical approaches to psychological change quite elegantly (1963, 1976), the resistance and control phenomena on which they are based seem to us much more ominous and ubiquitous in theory than in practice. In our view, this discrepancy exists because the expectation of therapeutic power battles is derived from questionable theoretical assumptions. These have relevance to the present chapter and bear further mention:

Circular Definition of Resistance

As Jacobson and Margolin (1979) have argued, resistance is always inferred from the behavior it attempts to explain. Why do clients fail to follow therapeutic directives? Resistance. How do you know they resist? Because they fail to follow therapeutic directives. In addition to biasing the clinician toward negative expectancies, this circular reasoning increases the tendency to overlook more specific reasons for the client's distress. We discuss these further below.

Unconscious Ideation

Several references to the unconscious can be found in writings on the paradoxical therapies (see, e.g., Haley, 1973). The hypothesis of unconscious functioning requires a second-order inference from the observed behavior to the presumed internal motivator, a "sign" approach to assessment and therapy that parallels traditional projective techniques (Goldfried, 1977).

The ostensibly unconscious phenomena Haley describes can be explained more parsimoniously by means of a social influence model (Barber, 1970; Ullmann & Krasner, 1975), and the cognitive contributors to such phenomena can be directly observed by the client (Mahoney, 1974). With this approach, the behavior, including affect and cognition, *is* the target and impels direct intervention without reference to underlying dynamic constructs.

Control as a Personality Variable

The notion of personality variables as stable, cross-situational qualities has been strongly criticized by many professionals (e.g., Krasner & Ullman, 1973; Mischel, 1968). Yet the concept of control as described by Haley and others bears great resemblance to this notion because the struggle to define interpersonal roles is assumed to generalize from the family to the therapist and to other relationships as well.

Another approach, which has greater experimental validation, views behavior in terms of the differential influence of situations (Ullmann & Krasner, 1975; Mischel, 1968). This view negates the assumption that compliance issues in therapy will always arise and explains how Ellis, with his remarkably powerful demeanor, can effect direct psychological change without resorting to paradoxical maneuvers.

Nearly any therapeutically relevant behavior, therefore, including resistance, merits reductionistic and comprehensive assessment to discover its causal contributors. Such assessment will sometimes confirm a cognitive set that is quite congruent with the notion of control—for example, "That therapist can't tell *me* what to do!"—and paradoxical maneuvers may then be appropriate. In other cases, however, the cognitive responses may not be at all controlling—and a complementary technique should then be applied (e.g., see the "Incorrect Bs," "Sabotaging the Counters," and "Denying Improvement" sections below). A client of the second author's, for instance, showed various kinds of resistance to treatment including missed sessions, anger at the therapist, refusal to do the homework or to do it correctly, and acute anxiety attacks following signs of therapeutic progress. Assessment revealed that each of these behaviors was influenced by a different set of cognitions, some of which were controlling and some of which were not:

1. I shouldn't have to work on this problem. It's society's fault anyway, so this isn't fair. I should work only on things that are my fault.
2. All this homework is a big hassle. I don't want to do it. I shouldn't do things I don't like.

3. I hate being told what to do. It reminds me of my father. I'm worthless if I do what anyone tells me.
4. When you [the therapist] show me how to analyze my thoughts, you're actually showing me how to criticize myself. But that means that you're criticizing me, and I can't stand to be treated that way. I'm worthless if somebody proves I'm wrong.
5. If I get over this problem, I'll be normal like everybody else and will lose my individuality. I need to be different to be happy.
6. If I get over this problem, I'll no longer be withdrawn. Then I'll be out in the open where I can be judged, and that scares the hell out of me. I'm worthless if everyone doesn't like me.
7. Therapy should go in three stages. The first stage is euphoria, introspection, and carefree frolic. The second stage is withdrawal and deep depression, retreating to the mountains to review the entire course of one's life. The third and final stage, a year later, is a last condemnation of all psychological bullshit and resolute striving towards one's goals. You [the therapist] are pushing me to get better now, and I'm barely into the second stage! Therapy must follow standard stages to work.

When clients have resistant beliefs that are not core beliefs, we may attempt to persuade, confront, and/or reinforce a more adaptive belief system and behavioral style. Core beliefs, however, because of their power, are often incorporated into a separate VCI or SP–SR hierarchy to allow a more systematic and repetitive attack. We use highly confrontational statements infrequently and only when a reinforcing therapeutic relationship has been established. This influences the client to think "He is criticizing my thinking because he wants the best for me" rather than "He is criticizing my thinking because I'm inadequate."

We add in this regard that clients are no different from anyone else. All people have difficulty changing their beliefs, and this difficulty is not necessarily a sign of unconscious resistance. Nearly any change, psychological or otherwise, will be difficult and uncomfortable at first. Both of the authors, for example, experienced several cognitive resistances when exposed to systematic desensitization as a therapeutic tool: "It's too mechanical"; "All these steps to memorize—what a drag"; "Therapy is supposed to be creative, so I shouldn't adopt someone else's procedure." We expect that many readers will have resistances to segments of this book. Some of these may be examined usefully as analogues to certain clients' perceptions of directive techniques.

CONTROL ISSUES

The interventions described in this section are utilized primarily when the client finds some aspect of the therapeutic relationship noxious. (Anxiety avoidance and other sources of noncompliance are discussed under separate headings.) A functional assessment usually reveals cognitions such as "I can't stand being told what to do"; "I'm worthless if I do what my therapist asks"; "I should have been able to solve my own problems"; "I have to prove my therapist wrong by failing to improve"; "Nobody can make me get better." One client, for instance, while learning VCI, was observed to tense her forearms, grit her teeth, frown, become flushed, and wrinkle her forehead. When asked to express her bodily feelings in words, she angrily stated, "I shouldn't have to do this! You're trying to put one over on me and make me a fool! I'll be damned if I'll do your techniques." A number of strategies to deal with this sort of problem are available. The first step is to realize that prognosis may not be as good for such people and that special techniques may be required.

Detachment of Therapist's Control

Cognitive assessment with the woman described in the preceding paragraph revealed that for her, using someone else's techniques brought on the feeling of being overwhelmed and helpless. The therapist decided to negotiate for self-modification of the procedures so that, in effect, the client gained much greater decision power over what interventions were used. She was also allowed to create minor variations in the VCI and SP–SR methodology so that the therapeutic procedures were perceived as "her techniques." These modifications lent her enough sense of control to withstand continued treatment, and the therapy was eventually successful.

Reality Confrontation

We use this technique primarily to persuade stubbornly resistant clients to continue in therapy long enough for the homework to take effect. The essence of the approach is to focus the client's attention on the realistic consequences of his or her resistant beliefs and behaviors. A good example of this approach, as used by Todd (1980) with resistant weight-loss clients, follows:

Therapist: I see that you didn't count your calories this week, and you didn't chart your eating behavior.

Client: No. I just couldn't do it.

T: Many people whom I have seen for weight problems get a little angry with me at first. They think, "Dr. Todd is oversimplifying my problems" or, "I have so few pleasures left in life as it is, and now he is trying to take away my food!"

C: Those thoughts did cross my mind.

T: I realize that charting is a tedious task, but if you can't do it, you don't have a ghost of a chance of losing weight. But consider this. There are tall people, short people, skinny people, fat people, all sorts of people, and this is perfectly all right. You could give up this weight-loss program, and then you could eat anything you like.

C: Oh no! I've made up my mind. I have to lose this weight.

T: Well, that's really great. Then this week you'll be willing to fill out these charts—

We would again emphasize that the techniques discussed in this section are only warranted if and when the assessment reveals a belief system that vitiates compliance with therapeutic directives. We do not view resistance as a universal phenomenon. Once the assessment of counter control is positive, a number of strategies are available to therapists in addition to those discussed formally here: They can encourage clients to continue resisting (e.g., Giles, 1979); they can predict clients' resistance before it occurs (Giles, 1979), or they can incorporate target cognitions into VCI or SP–SR. A gamut of paradoxical strategies, formats, and procedures have been described by Haley (1973, 1976).

We use these techniques primarily to persuade the client to continue in treatment and to do the homework. Once this bridge has been crossed, such maneuvers become unnecessary. If the client performs VCI and SP–SR diligently and without sabotage, the therapy is successful 99 percent of the time.

Shaping

This technique is applicable to clients who refuse initially to "take responsibility" for their problems. Adolescent clients, for example, will often insist on blaming other people for their plight and will not easily tolerate the implication that their thinking is contributing to the difficulty. With such cases, we often take two to four sessions to teach A–B–C theory *solely as it relates to other people:*

T: Your dad thinks that *you* are making him mad by keeping your room a mess. But a messy room is an A, and As don't cause emotions, Bs do. What do you think he might be saying to himself to get so hot and bothered over all this?

For homework, we have the client observe for several weeks how other people's beliefs make them miserable. In this way, the eventual transition to personal issues becomes easier to tolerate.

SABOTAGING THE COUNTERS

Nearly every client argues against the therapeutic self-statements used in the VCI and the SP–SR techniques, but this behavior usually stops within 7 to 10 days. If it does not, we use the *sabotage counter* technique (Loudis, 1979). The client writes the irrational B and its counter and then the sabotage or argument to this counter, followed by a statement that negates the sabotage. This process is continued until all the sabotages are listed and their counters produced. For homework, the client writes the irrational B on one side of a notecard. On the other side are listed all the arguments against any of the sabotages that might occur. The card is reviewed until the counters are sufficiently established in memory to incorporate them into the VCI procedure. For example, a card might contain the following statement:

Irrational B: I'm worthless if I can't fix my car.
Counter: Nonsense, worthlessness has nothing to do with it!
Sabotage: But every man I know can fix a car, so I must be less than a man.
Counter: Fixing a car is a learned skill and does not measure masculinity.
Sabotage: But if my friends find out I can't fix a car, they will make fun of me.
Counter: It's no big deal if they do. I can certainly take a joke once in a while.

CRISIS INTERVENTION

Crisis intervention is usually handled with the *perceptual shift* technique. Perceptual shift (McMullin, Assafi, & Chapman, 1978) is designed to address multiple irrational beliefs simultaneously and may be used to supplement or replace VCI and SP–SR in weekly homework sessions. (Almost all of our clients learn this technique.) It is especially useful for crisis situations because multiple Bs (seven or more) of varied precepts are usually involved. Contrary to the VCI and SP–SR techniques, whose therapeutic potential lies mainly in repetition, perceptual shift works by means of a rapid accumulation of *bridge thoughts* (explained below), whereby irrational beliefs, especially in crisis, can be suddenly and dramatically overcome and emotional trauma relieved.

During a crisis, the therapist should employ the perceptual shift technique directly, authoritatively, and confidently so as to lend structure and control to the situation. Statements such as—"Tell me exactly what has happened"; "Go get a pencil and a sheet of paper"; "I'm sure that belief is irrational"—all exemplify this demeanor. Perceptual shift is a written technique and involves five steps, which are addressed in the following order:

Step 1: The client gets a sheet of paper and divides it lengthwise into four columns (see Appendix F). In the first column, he lists all of the Bs as they occur in the situation. The therapist assists in this process by asking exploratory questions until the list is complete.

Step 2: The client judges the listed beliefs as true or false and writes each verdict in the second column. If the client cannot make these judgments easily, the therapist directs him or her through one of the logical analysis techniques discussed in Chapter 8.

Step 3: In the third column, the client lists a general counter for each of the listed beliefs.

Step 4: The client comes up with reasons, images, memories, logical arguments, emotions, perceptions, and/or beliefs from his or her experience as to why each of the general counters is true. Ten or more of these details, or referents, per counter are optimal. As a reminder, the client writes a description of each of these details in the fourth column. Referents will often show considerable overlap from one counter to the next (see Figure 13–1).

Step 5: The client addresses the first counter on the list and concentrates on memorizing and visualizing each of its referents until all have come clearly to mind for a minute or longer. Each of the succeeding counters is addressed, in the same fashion, until the list is complete.

A (situation): I overheard a friend criticizing me.
C (emotion): Sad and depressed

B	True or False	General Counter	Details of Counters
Everybody must like me.	False	A person can be happy even if people dislike him or her.	List all the public figures I know who are happy despite being disliked by thousands of people.
			Think of 10 situations where I made myself miserable trying to get people to like me.
			Meditate about all the times I got over not having a specific person like me.
			Write the names of all the people I know who have more friends than I but who still feel unhappy and have problems.

Fig. 13–1. An example of a client's perpetual shift worksheet. (Adapted from *Straight Talk to Parents* by R. McMullin, I. Assafi, & S. Chapman. Lakewood, Colorado: Counseling Research Institute, 1978, p. 56.)

The therapist guides the client through Step 4, gives directions and preliminary practice with Step 5, and asks the client to call back after completing the list (or immediately, if a problem or question should arise). Although one client took five hours to complete this assignment, most do so within two hours and call back feeling greatly relieved. The cumulative reexperiencing of new and overlapping referents, usually by the eighth general counter, creates momentum towards a "shift" in cognitive processes that can dramatically alter irrational Bs and their emotional traumata.

The following abbreviated example demonstrates the use of the perceptual shift technique by a client whose husband had left her two days earlier. It was this event that led to the crisis call.

Step 1: First belief on this list: I need to depend on my husband to be happy. It will be terrible, and I can't survive without him.
Step 2: Judgment: False
Step 3: General counter: I can take care of myself and do everything that is important in life even if he is not around.
Step 4: There were numerous examples of past and present activities the client had successfully performed in her husband's absence: for example, called the plumber when the pipes broke, took the car to a garage for repair, worked full-time in a clothing store, volunteered in the community, kept the checkbook, and took art classes.

Some of this client's other beliefs were:

1. I'm not sexual.
2. I have failed in this marriage. It's all my fault.
3. I will never find another man.
4. I don't have what it takes to be a good wife.
5. I'm terribly lonely.
6. He may never come back.
7. I have to do anything I can to get him back.
8. I must have done something to drive him away.

For true Bs, clients are instructed to use the third column of Appendix F to list assertive coping behaviors to deal with the situation. Beliefs numbers 5 and 6 of client discussed above were rated true. All of the other beliefs were handled by challenging the thoughts.

The perceptual shift technique can be used not only in crisis intervention and weekly homework sessions, but in working on particularly difficult hierarchy items in VCI.

DENYING IMPROVEMENT

Because improvement usually occurs gradually with cognitive restructuring therapy, clients often do not realize that they are getting better. They may even deny obvious improvement because they are so accustomed to focusing on their own faults and shortcomings and on those of others. We counter this problem by gathering extensive behavioral data before treatment begins and as it progresses. A series of weekly note sheets using the SORKC assessment equation (see Chapter 4) is very helpful in this regard. We emphasize the recording of extensive behavioral data with two therapist–client dialogues below:

> **C:** My wife says I'm not getting any better, and I feel as though she is right.
>
> **T:** Well, maybe so. Let me review my notes from 10 weeks ago when we began. You were too terrified to go into the supermarket or to drive on the freeways. You wanted to ask for a raise at work but didn't know what to say. You were also very afraid of your boss and would work overtime for him even if you didn't feel like it. You rated your anxiety at 9 SUDs in these situations and felt substantially depressed and inadequate over your seeming inability to conquer your fears.
>
> My notes from a week ago suggest that you have done a superb job in making changes in your life. You enter supermarkets and drive on the freeways several times a week and report only minimal anxiety while doing so. You asked your boss for a raise and got it, and you have refused to work overtime on three occasions when it was not convenient. And I would assume that your sense of inadequacy about your fears has diminished since you have substantially conquered them. Am I misinterpreting any of this?
>
> **C:** No, I realize now that you're right. I really have done a great deal for myself, and I feel pretty good about it.
> It's just that a few problems remain, and I spend much of my time mulling over them.
>
> **T:** Well, then, let's talk not only about those remaining problems but also about your tendency to focus on the negatives without giving equal time to the considerable number of good things in your life.

> **T:** And what were the SUDs this week?
>
> **C:** Still at 8. Exactly where they were when I started this VCI stuff.
>
> **T:** I'm not so sure. According to my notes, your anxiety was so bad that you couldn't sleep, you had constant diarrhea, and you would sweat and shake before each presentation at work. As of this week, you were sleeping well, had no diarrhea, and you had not fallen apart at the last speaking engagement.

C: But I still have anxiety.
T: Our memory of anxiety is never as bad as what we are experiencing in the present. From now on, I would like you to rate the SUDs relative to what these situations were like a month ago.

Improvement scores on our standard post-tests are also helpful in this regard (see Chapter 3).

WORKING ON IRRELEVANT Bs

In some instances, therapists unwittingly may be trying to change Bs that are irrelevant to their clients' distress. A therapist may suspect that this problem has arisen when one or more of the following signals are present:

1. The client no longer believes the cognitions that seemed to be causing the problem, but the negative affect remains.
2. Previously undiscovered Bs continue to appear in place of those no longer believed.
3. The therapist has an uncomfortable feeling that he or she has not discovered the true problem cognitions and is working instead on irrelevant ones.

The problem of irrelevant Bs occurs when the therapist has failed to assess all the Bs in the proper A–B–C sequence of conditioning. Although only the A–B–C sequence is explained to the client, the actual influence of mediational cognitions is more complex. The following complete formula demonstrates that cognitions intervene through a *stimulus–emotion–behavior* chain:

$$B_0 \rightarrow A \rightarrow B_1 \rightarrow C^1_{emo} \rightarrow B_2 \rightarrow C^2_{emo} \rightarrow B_3 \rightarrow C_{beh} \rightarrow B_4$$

where

B_0 = A belief about an environmental event that has not yet occurred. The B sensitizes the client to certain negative aspects of A. For example, "She will reject me if I ask her to dance"; "I'm going to fail this test if there are a lot of questions."

A = Environmental event (stimulus). For example, woman refuses to dance with client, client fails exam.

B_1	=	A belief or evaluation of the event. For example, "It's horrible that she rejected me"; "I'm worthless because I failed this exam."
C^1_{emo}	=	First emotional response. For example, fear, depression, guilt, anger.
B_2	=	An evaluation of the emotions. For example, "It's dangerous to be anxious. I could go crazy. I might lose control of this anger and go into a rage. Feeling this way means I am very sick. I may have a breakdown."
C^2_{emo}	=	Second emotional response produced by B_2s. For example, fear is built to panic, sadness becomes deep depression.
B_3	=	A judgment about how to reduce the C_2 emotions. For example, "I have to go to the hospital"; "I must reach my therapist"; "I must punch somebody when I feel this angry."
C_{beh}	=	The behavioral response the client makes. For example, calls the therapist, goes to the hospital.
B_4	=	A judgment about the behavioral consequences of one's own action. For example, "I must be really sick to go to the hospital"; "My therapist must really be disgusted with me for calling so late."

The therapeutic importance of assessing all the Bs can be demonstrated by the following example: A client of the first author had panic attacks whenever she had to drive on freeways. She reduced this anxiety from 10 to 7 SUDs by working on her Bs, but the anxiety was not further reduced until her other cognitions (B_0 to B_4) were extinguished. The client's stimulus–emotion–behavior chain associated with her freeway phobia was as follows:

B_0	=	I always panic on freeways.
A	=	Client enters a freeway.
B_1	=	"I'm trapped, this is dangerous."
C^1_{emo}	=	Tension and fear.
B_2	=	"I'm getting anxious. I can't control this fear, and I may faint. I'm going to fall to pieces."
C^2_{emo}	=	Panic attack.
B_3	=	"I must escape and get help to reduce my panic."
C_{beh}	=	Client drives to an emergency room for tranquilizers.

B_4 = "I am weak and gutless. I must be really sick to go to a hospital just because I'm a little tense."

The B_0 . . . B_4 analysis gives the therapist greater opportunity to discover the exact beliefs that are contributing to the problem so that the VCI and SP–SR techniques can be effective. If multiple Bs are found using this technique, the perceptual shift technique becomes the intervention of choice.

PROCEDURES WITH CLIENTS OF LOW ABSTRACT INTELLIGENCE

Clients with low abstract intelligence as measured by standard intelligence tests are given the checklist analysis (Chapter 8) as the sole method of analyzing their Bs. (They are not able to grasp the linguistic technique.) We help them grasp additional therapeutic concepts by employing as many concrete techniques as possible. The script for the VCI and SP–SR techniques is written, and each hierarchy item is graphically described on a separate notecard. We also use tape recordings of various interventions to supplement this procedure and keep our language in the sessions more free of psychological jargon and abstract terminology.

VARIANTS OF VCI AND SP–SR

Variants become necessary for two reasons. First, the client often satiates with the VCI and SP–SR techniques after several weeks, and negative affect may subsequently become conditioned to the techniques. Second, because of client idiosyncrasies, certain variations increase the effectiveness of the procedures.

All variations are congruent with the basic principles of VCI and SP–SR. With the standard versions, repetition of the imagined A–B sequence is paired with an adaptive stimulus to produce the therapeutic effect. The variations increase the number of adaptive stimuli available to the therapist and are limited only to his or her imagination.

We have successfully used the following variations: relaxation, realistic thoughts versus counters (Ellis, 1974), pleasant images (Kroger & Fezler, 1976); decrease in pulse rate, EMG reduction, covert sensitization (Cautela, 1967); assertive imagery, covert models (Kazdin, 1974); and premacking of coverants (Todd, 1972).

TERMINATION

Termination occurs when the client's major presenting complaints have been relieved and appropriate analysis, maintenance, and self-intervention techniques have been learned. We often will leave the client with one or more problems to overcome alone in order to save time and expense and to give the client practice using the techniques without the therapist's assistance. We then schedule a maintenance appointment for a month later.

Most clients are seen for follow-up interviews and post-testing six months and a year following treatment. We encourage clients to keep in touch with us by phone at bimonthly intervals in order to track continued progress and maintenance gains. We tell them that therapy does not guarantee a problem-free existence but builds skills for coping with problems. If they have a bad day or series of days, they are to examine whether or not irrational Bs are becoming problematic and begin the techniques of VCI, SP–SR, their variants, or perceptual shift if appropriate. If, however, clients have two or more weeks of continued misery in spite of their efforts, they are to call and schedule an appointment.

Any other doubts, hesitancies, and/or success stories that the client wants to share at the termination interview are welcomed and discussed.

14

Cognitive Restructuring Therapy in Groups

Cognitive restructuring therapy was originally developed for group work at Jefferson County Mental Health Center, by author McMullin and his associate Casey, and was adapted for individual treatment five years later. The Jefferson County Mental Health Center is known in the Denver area for its difficult, multiple-problem clientele, and many of the original CRT groups were piloted (as a last resort) on the most difficult members of this population. A large percentage of clients in the very first CRT groups failed to improve. They had learned from years of experience to outmaneuver standard therapeutic protocol, and a highly structured, highly educational approach was subsequently developed to undercut their sabotages. Fairly extensive data on this approach (McMullin & Coolbaugh, 1977) indicated the following success rates:

Worsened	0%
Failed to improve or improved only moderately	10%
Dropped out	10%
Improved significantly	80%

Casey and McMullin (1976) developed a cognitive treatment package that delineates step-by-step procedures for using CRT in groups. The package includes photographic slides, a treatment manual, and a booklet for clients (McMullin & Casey's *Talk Sense to Yourself*). The present chapter will not reiterate Casey and McMullin's work but will supplement it with a discussion of differences between CRT for groups and CRT for individuals. We will discuss these differences under the headings of "Structural Adaptations to Groups" and "Increasing Therapeutic Control."

In general, group CRT is equally or more effective than its individual counterpart for problems that are not particularly unusual or complicated. With these cases, it usually is faster and cheaper than individual treatment and affords much less opportunity for "game playing" and sabotage. Individual CRT, however, lends itself more to complicated situations and to treatment obstacles such as irrelevant Bs and failure with logical analysis, and it is often more suitable to the clinical situations many therapists face.

STRUCTURAL ADAPTATIONS TO GROUPS

The CRT groups at Jefferson County Mental Health Center consisted of 30 people divided into six "small" groups of five members each. Each small group had one facilitator. Since the small group is an effective therapeutic unit, a facility using the CRT approach could presumably handle numerous participants at a time.

The therapists' materials include a 35-millimeter projector, an overhead projector, a blackboard, and Casey and McMullin's (1976) group therapy package. Clients are required to bring a notebook for use for homework.

Each CRT course consists of 10 sessions, each lasting two hours, and each meeting follows a highly structured schedule of events (Casey & McMullin, 1976). Adherence to the structured format is extremely important—the therapist(s) and facilitators meet 30 minutes prior to each group to rehearse the procedures—and means to prevent group sidetracking and detouring are frequently used (see the next section). If a group member becomes too upset to continue, he or she is quietly escorted by the facilitator to a separate room to talk about the difficulty. The facilitator returns to the group after a short while; the client is free to return to the group when ready.

Although each participant is expected to help others and to participate in the exercises, no one is required to tell the group about personal problems. The hierarchies, logical analyses, and some other procedures are done as homework so that only the therapists and facilitators have ready access to this information. A beneficial mixed-group effect is consistently found; consequently, all groups are heterogeneous in terms of such variables as age, sex, and presenting problem. When groups are homogenous—for example, all alcoholics, all depressive, all men, or all women—

clients have greater difficulty recognizing the irrationality of other group members' Bs and begin reinforcing each other for maladaptive cognitions.

We set aside 30 minutes to address individual problems after each group. When the 10 sessions are concluded, any clients who need more CRT are scheduled for appointments contingent on their completing required homework.

INCREASING THERAPEUTIC CONTROL

The proper use of group cohesion and group pressure can overcome many of the resistances to treatment that are characteristic of difficult clinical populations. The small groups keep the same members throughout the entire course. At the first meeting, each group picks a name for itself; this exercise relaxes the participants and strengthens group cohesion. The initial 15 minutes of each session are used for chatting and small talk. The facilitators strongly encourage group pressure toward doing the homework, talking in A–B–C terminology, and using the counters to effect personal change. If two group members begin a session by reporting on their homework assignment or recounting a success story, the rest of the group will feel impelled to do likewise. The facilitator praises compliance or extinguishes comments that are sidetracking or not oriented toward CRT.

The therapist(s) remain task-oriented throughout every session. No formal breaks are allowed during the first five meetings. Before this policy was made, group members would invariably get together and reinforce each other for noncompliance: for example, "But this isn't like T.A.!" or "I don't believe any of this stuff! Do you?" Group CRT is unlike individual treatment in that both personal catharsis and complaints of failure experiences are extinguished in the group, and only reports of success are reinforced:

> **Therapist:** Who had some successes this week?
>
> **Client:** I really tried to do the homework, but my daughter is upsetting me so much that nothing seemed to work.
>
> **T:** Okay. We will help you figure that out in a minute when we discuss A–B–C theory. Now, who had some successes this week?

The facilitators collect homework at the beginning of every session. They mark it, make comments, and return it to the client the next week. A "guarantee" card is handed to each member at the first session which is signed by the therapist and by the client. The card reads, "We guarantee that you will not get any better until after the sixth session."

Finally, several reinforcement procedures are used to enhance group motivation. McMullin and Casey ran CRT groups so often that they developed a routine that participants enjoyed: each completed homework assignment earns "funny money" equal to a real dollar that can then be deducted from the client's fee. And success stories, completed assignments, and attendance are amply praised. Each session ends on a positive note: "Next week we are *really* going to learn something special." And the last session of the course is celebrated with a potluck party that participants arrange.

TRAINING THERAPISTS FOR GROUP CRT

Many therapists around the country have become interested in group CRT and have been supervised in this approach in the following manner. They act as group facilitators in one full class period (10 sessions) and then run two or more classes alone while author McMullin observes. Treatment success rates recorded during one training session were as follows (McMullin & Coolbaugh, 1977):

First session alone: 55 percent significantly improved
Second session: 68 percent significantly improved
Third session: 80 percent significantly improved

The foregoing figures suggest that the trainees gained effectiveness through continued practice with the treatment approach. This continuous improvement reflects the importance of fine points in CRT. Hopefully, the material in this and other chapters will have explained these fine points sufficiently for other clinicians to bypass many of the frustrations and pitfalls of trial and error learning and experience alone.

References

Abramson, E. *Behavioral approaches to weight control*. New York: W. W. Norton, 1976.

Aronson, E. *The social animal*. San Francisco, California: W. H. Freeman, 1972.

Arthur, A. Z. Psychology as engineering and technology of behavior. *Canadian Psychologist*, 1971, *12*, 30–36.

Arthur, A. Z. Theory—and action-oriented research. *Journal of Clinical and Consulting Psychology*, 1972, *38*, 129–133.

Azrin, N. H. & Nunn, R. G. *Habit control in a day*. New York: Pocket Books, 1978.

Bailey, C. *Fit or fat?* Boston, Mass.: Houghton Mifflin, 1978.

Bandler, R. & Grinder, J. *The structure of magic*. Palo Alto, California: Science and Behavior, 1975.

Bandura, A. Vicarious processes: A case of no-trial learning. In L. Berkowitz (Ed.), *Advances in experimental social psychology* (Vol. 2). New York: Academic Press, 1965.

Bandura, A. *Principles of behavior modification*. New York: Holt, Rienhart, and Winston, 1969.

Bandura, A. *Social learning theory*. Englewood Cliffs, New Jersey: Prentice Hall, 1977. (a)

Bandura, A. Self-efficacy: Towards a unifying theory of behavior change. *Psychological Review*, 1977, *84*, 191–215. (b)

Barber, T. X. *Suggested ("hypnotic") behavior: The trance paradigm versus an alternative paradigm*. Harding, Mass.: Medfield Foundation, 1970.

Beck, A. *Cognitive therapy and the emotional disorders*. New York: New American Library, 1976.

Beck, A., Rush, A., Shaw, B., & Emery, G. *Cognitive therapy of depression.* New York: Guilford, 1979.

Bolles, R. C. Learning, motivation, and cognition. In W. Estes (Ed.), *Handbook of learning and cognitive processes.* New York: Halsted, 1975.

Breger, L. & McGaugh, Jr. Critique and reformulation of "learning theory": Approaches to psychotherapy, and neurosis. *Psychological Bulletin* 1965, *63,* 338–358.

Breland, K. & Breland, M. The misbehavior of organisms. *American Psychologist,* 1961, *16,* 681–684.

Brewer, W. There is no convincing evidence for operant or classical conditioning in adult humans. In W. Weiner and D. Palermo (Eds.), *Cognition and the symbolic processes.* New York: Halsted, 1974.

Cameron, R. The clinical implementation of behavior change techniques: A cognitively oriented conceptualization of therapeutic "compliance" and "resistance." In J. Foreyt and D. Rathjen (Eds.), *Cognitive behavior therapy: Research and application.* New York: Plenum, 1978.

Casey, W. & McMullin, R. *Cognitive-restructuring therapy package.* Lakewood, Colorado: Counseling Research Institute, 1976.

Cautela, J. Covert sensitization. *Psychological Reports,* 1967, *20,* 459–468.

Cautela, J. Covert negative reinforcement. *Journal of Behavioral Therapy and Experimental Psychiatry,* 1970, *1,* 273–278.

Cautela, J., Walsh, K., & Wish, P. The use of covert reinforcement in the modification of attitudes towards the mentally retarded. *Journal of Psychology,* 1971, *77,* 257–260.

Chomsky, N. A review of Skinner's Verbal Behavior. *Language,* 1959, *35,* 26–58.

DiLoretto, A. *Comparative psychotherapy.* New York: Aldine-Atherton, 1971.

Domjan, M. & Wilson, N. Contribution of ingestive behaviors to taste aversion learning. *Journal of Comparative and Physiological Psychology,* 1968, *65,* 8–12.

Ellis, A. *Reason and emotion in psychotherapy.* New York: Lyle Stuart, 1962.

Ellis, A. *Humanistic psychotherapy.* New York: McGraw-Hill, 1974.

Ellis, A. *Growth through reason.* Hollywood, California: Wilshire, 1975.

Ellis, A. Personal communication, 1978.

Ellis, A. & Harper, R. *A new guide to rational living.* Hollywood, California: Wilshire, 1978.

Eysenck, H. *The dynamics of anxiety and hysteria.* London: Routledge and Kegan Paul, 1957.

Foreyt, J. & Rathjen, D. (Eds.). *Cognitive behavior therapy: Research and application.* New York: Plenum, 1978.

Garcia, J. & Koelling, R. Relation of cue to consequence in avoidance learning. *Psychonomic Science,* 1966, *4,* 123–124.

Giles, T. R. Some principles of intervention in the absence of therapeutic alliance. *Transactional Analysis Journal,* 1979, *9,* 294–296.

Goldfried, M. Behavioral assessment in perspective. In J. Cone and R. Hawkins (Eds.), *Behavioral assessment*. New York: Brunner/Mazel, 1977.

Guthrie, E. R. *The psychology of learning*. New York: Harper, 1935.

Haley, J. *Strategies of psychotherapy*. New York: Grune & Stratton, 1963.

Haley, J. *Uncommon therapy: The psychiatric techniques of Milton H. Erickson, M.D*. New York: Norton, 1973.

Haley, J. *Problem-solving therapy*. San Francisco, California: Jossey-Bass, 1976.

Hite, S. *The Hite report*. New York: Dell, 1976.

Hollon, S. & Beck, A. Cognitive therapy of depression. In P. Kendall and S. Hollon (Eds), *Cognitive-behavioral interventions*. New York: Academic Press, 1979.

Hovland, C. & Weiss, W. The influence of source credibility on communication effectiveness. *Public Opinion Quarterly*, 1951, *15*, 635–650.

Husted, J. Desensitization procedures in dealing with female sexual dysfunction. *The Counseling Psychologist*, 1975, *5*, 30–37.

Jacobson, N. & Margolin, G. *Marital therapy*. New York: Brunner/Mazel, 1979.

Kamin, L. J. Predictability, surprise, attention and conditioning. In B. A. Campbell & R. M. Church (Eds.), *Punishment and aversive behavior*. New York: Appleton-Century-Crofts, 1969.

Kanfer, F. & Phillips, J. *Learning foundations of behavior therapy*. New York: John Wiley, 1970.

Kazdin, A. Covert modeling, model similarity, and reduction of avoidance behavior. *Behavior Therapy*, 1974, *5*, 325–340.

Kazdin, A. & Wilcoxin, L. Systematic desensitization and nonspecific treatment effects: A methodological evaluation. *Psychological Bulletin*, 1976, *83*(5), 729–758.

Kendall, P. & Hollon, S. (Eds.), *Cognitive-behavioral interventions*. New York: Academic Press, 1979.

Kendall, P. & Korgeski, G. Assessment of cognitive and behavioral interventions. *Cognitive Therapy and Research*, 1979, *3*, 1–21.

Krasner, L. & Ullmann, L. *Behavior influence and personality*. New York: Holt, Rinehart, and Winston, 1973

Kroger, W. & Fezler, W. *Hypnosis and behavior modification: Imagery conditioning*. Philadelphia, Pennsylvania: Lippincott, 1976.

Lasser, N., Ingvar, D., & Skinhoj, E. Brain function and blood flow. *Scientific American*, 1978, 62–71.

Lazarus, A. A. *Behavior therapy and beyond*. New York: McGraw-Hill, 1971.

Lenneberg, E. *The biological foundations of language*. New York: John Wiley, 1967.

Lewinsohn, P., Biglan, A., & Zeiss, A. Behavioral treatment of depression. In P. Davidson (Ed.), *The behavioral management of anxiety, depression, and pain*. New York: Brunner/Mazel, 1976.

Linder, E., Cooper, J., & Jones, E. Decision freedom as a determinant of the role of incentive magnitude in attitude change. *Journal of Personality and Social Psychology,* 1967, *6,* 245–254.

London, P. The end of ideology in behavior modification. *American Psychologist,* 1972, *27,* 913–920.

Loudis, L. Personal communication, 1979.

Mahoney, M. *Cognition and behavior modification.* Cambridge, Mass.: Ballinger, 1974.

Mahoney, M. & Mahoney, K. *Permanent weight control.* New York: W. W. Norton, 1976.

Maier, S. F. Failure to escape traumatic shock: Incompatible skeletal motor responses or learned helplessness? *Learning and Motivation,* 1970, *1,* 157–170.

Maltzman, I. Theoretical conceptions of semantic conditioning and generalization. In T. R. Dixon & D. L. Horton (Eds.), *Verbal behavior and general behavior theory.* Englewood Cliffs, New Jersey: Prentice Hall, 1968.

Marks, I. Cognitive behavior therapy in the treatment of phobic and obsessive compulsive disorders. In D. Meichenbaum (Ed.), *Cognitive behavior therapy: A practical guide.* New York: BMA Publications, 1978.

Maultsby, M. *Handbook of rational self-counseling.* Madison, Wisconsin: Association for Rational Thinking, 1971.

Maultsby, M. *More personal happiness through rational self-counseling.* Madison, Wisconsin: Association for Rational Thinking, 1974.

McLean, P. Therapeutic decision-making in the treatment of depression. In P. Davidson (Ed.), *The behavioral management of anxiety, depression, and pain.* New York: Brunner/Mazel, 1976.

McMullin, R., Assafi, I., & Chapman, S. *Straight talk to parents.* Lakewood, Colorado: Counseling Research Institute, 1978.

McMullin, R. & Casey, W. *Talk sense to yourself.* Lakewood, Colorado: Counseling Research Institute, 1975.

McMullin, R. & Coolbaugh, C. *Lakewood research report.* Lakewood, Colorado: Jefferson County Mental Health Center, 1977.

Meichenbaum, D. *Cognitive-behavior modification.* New York: Plenum, 1977.

Millenson, J. & Leslie, J. *Principles of behavioral analysis.* New York: Macmillan, 1979.

Mischel, N. *Personality and assessment.* New York: John Wiley, 1968.

Nash, J. & Long, L. *Taking charge of your weight and well-being.* Palo Alto, California: W. H. Freeman, 1978.

Razran, G. The observable unconscious and the inferable conscious in Soviet psychophysiology. *Psychological Review,* 1961, *68,* 81–147.

Rescorla, R. & Wagner, A. A theory of Pavlovian conditioning: Variations in the effectiveness of reinforcement and non-reinforcement. In H. H. Black & W. F. Prokasy (Eds.), *Classical Conditioning II.* New York: Appleton-Century-Crofts, 1972.

Schwartz, B. *The psychology of learning and behavior*. New York: W. W. Norton, 1978.

Seligman, M. On the generality of the laws of learning. *Psychological Review*, 1970, *77*, 406–418.

Seligman, M. Phobias and preparedness. *Behavior Therapy*, 1971, *2*, 307–320.

Seligman, M. *Helplessness*. San Francisco, California: W. H. Freeman, 1975.

Sherif, M. & Hovland, C. *Social judgment: Assimilation and contrast effects in communication and attitude changes*. New Haven, Connecticut: Yale University Press, 1961.

Shettleworth, S. J. Constraints on learning. In D. Lehrman, R. Hinde, and E. Shaw (Eds.), *Advances in the study of behavior*. (Vol. 4). New York: Academic Press, 1972.

Skinner, B. F. 'Superstition' in the pigeon. *Journal of Experimental Psychology*, 1948, *38*, 168–172.

Skinner, B. F. *About behaviorism*. New York: Alfred Knopf, 1974.

Slobin, D. (Ed.). *The ontogenesis of grammar*. New York: Academic Press, 1971.

Snygg, D. & Combs, A. *Individual behavior*. New York: Harper, 1949.

Spielberger, J. *State-trait anxiety inventory*. Palo Alto, California: Consulting Psychology Press, 1969.

Staats, A. W. *Learning language, and cognition*. New York: Holt, Rinehart, and Winston, 1968.

Staddon, J. & Simmelhag, V. The "superstition experiment": A reexamination of its implications for the principles of adaptive behavior. *Psychological Review*, 1971, *78*, 3–43.

Steger, J. Cognitive behavioral strategies in the treatment of sexual problems. In J. Foreyt & D. Rathjen (Eds.), *Cognitive behavior therapy: Research and application*, New York: Plenum, 1978.

Stuart, R. & Davis, B. *Slim chance in a fat world*. Champaign, Illinois: Research Press, 1972.

Sutherland, E., Amit Z., & Weiner, A. *Phobia Free: How to fight your fears*. New York: Stein and Day, 1977.

Thorndike, E. L. *Animal intelligence*. New York: Macmillan, 1911.

Todd, F. Coverant control of self-evaluative responses in the treatment of depression: A new use for an old principle. *Behavior Therapy*, 1972, *3*, 91–94.

Todd, F. Personal communication, 1980.

Turk, D. Cognitive behavioral techniques in the management of pain. In J. Foreyt & D. Rathjen (Eds.), *Cognitive behavior therapy: Research and application*. New York: Plenum, 1978.

Ullmann, L. & Krasner, L. *A psychological approach to abnormal behavior*. Englewood Cliffs, New Jersey: Prentice-Hall, 1975.

Walster, E., Aronson, E., & Abrahams, D. On increasing the persuasiveness of a low prestige communicator. *Journal of Experimental and Social Psychology*. 1966, *2*, 325–342.

Watson, J. B. *Behavior: An introduction to comparative psychology*. New York: Holt, 1914.

Watson, J. S. Memory and "contingency analysis" in infant learning. *Merrill-Palmer Quarterly*, 1971, *13*, 55–76. (a)

Watson, J. S. Cognitive-perceptual development in infancy: Setting for the seventies. *Merrill-Palmer Quarterly*, 1971, *13*, 139–152. (b)

Williams, D. & Williams H. Auto-maintenance in the pigeon: Sustained pecking despite contingent non-reinforcement. *Journal of the Experimental Analysis of Behavior*, 1969, *12*, 511–520.

Wilson, G. T. Cognitive behavior therapy: Paradigm shift or passing phase? In J. Foreyt & D. Rathjen (Eds.), *Cognitive behavior therapy: Research and application*. New York: Plenum, 1978.

Wilson, J. *Language and the pursuit of truth*. London: Cambridge University Press, 1956.

Wolpe, J. *Psychotherapy by reciprocal inhibition*. Stanford: Stanford University Press, 1958.

Wolpe, J. *The practice of behavior therapy*. New York: Pergaman Press, 1969.

Wolpe, J. *The practice of behavior therapy*. New York: Pergamon Press, 1973.

Wolpe, J. Personal communication, 1981.

Yates, A. *Theory and practice in behavior therapy*. New York: Wiley, 1975.

Zilbergeld, B. *Male Sexuality*. New York: Bantam, 1978.

Zung, W. A self-rating depression scale. *Archives of General Psychiatry*, 1965, 63–70.

Appendices

Appendix A
Thoughts That Cause Problems

1. People must love me or I will be miserable.
2. Making mistakes is terrible.
3. People should be condemned for their wrongdoing.
4. It is terrible when things go wrong.
5. My emotions can't be controlled.
6. I should be terribly worried about threatening situations.
7. Self discipline is *too* hard to achieve.
8. I *must* depend on others.
9. My childhood must always affect me.
10. I can't stand the way others act.
11. There is a perfect solution.
12. I should be better than others.
13. If others criticize me, I did something wrong.
14. I can't change what I think.
15. I should help everyone who needs it.
16. I must never show any weakness.
17. Healthy people don't get upset.
18. There is one true love.
19. I should never hurt anyone.
20. There is a magic cure.
21. The therapist must help me, it's his job.
22. Strong people don't ask for help.

23. I can do things when I'm in the mood.
24. Possible is the same as probable.
25. I am inferior.
26. I am always in the spotlight.
27. People ought to do what I wish.
28. Giving up is the best policy.
29. I need to be sure to decide.
30. One must have guarantees.
31. Change is unnatural.
32. Knowing "why" is essential.
33. People should trust me.
34. I should be happy all the time.
35. There is a sinister, dangerous part of me.
36. Working on my problems could hurt me.
37. The world ought to be fair.
38. I am not responsible for my behavior.
39. It is always better not to be genuine.
40. I have no problems.
41. Anxiety is dangerous.
42. You can't tell me anything about me that I don't know.
43. People shouldn't act the way they do.
44. I should be able to control my kids (or spouse's) behavior.
45. Willpower alone can solve all my problems.

Appendix B
Checklist Analysis

A (the external situation): ______________________________

____

B (my thought or beliefs about A): ______________________

____

C (my emotion and behavior in response to A): ____________

____

		Circle One	
1.	Does the belief make me feel better?	Yes	No
2.	Does the belief help me accomplish my goals?	Yes	No
3.	Does the belief help me get along with others?	Yes	No
4.	Would everybody have the same belief in this situation?	Yes	No
5.	Do I always feel this way in similar situations	Yes	No

____

Total Yes ________

Total No ________

Appendix C

Hierarchy Type A

Write down 10 situations (A) in which your emotion (C) occurs. For each situation write your thought or attitude (B) about it. Write A and B pairs in the order of intensity of C: 1 is the lowest intensity; 10 is the highest. At zero, write a situation and thought not connected with any emotion at all.

SUD
Scale

0 A ______________________________

____

B ______________________________

____

---

1 A ______________________________

____

B ______________________________

____

---

2 A ______________________________

____

B ______________________________

____

3 A

B

4 A

B

5 A

B

6 A

B

7 A

B

8 A

B

9 A

B

10 A

B

Appendix D

Hierarchy Type B

Least believable thought: ______________________________

____

____

Situation 1 (low SUD)

A ______________________________

____

C ______________________________

____

Situation 2 (medium SUD)

A ______________________________

____

C ______________________________

____

Situation 3 (high SUD)

A ______________________________

____

C ______________________________

____

Moderately believable thought: ____________________

____

____

Situation 1 (low SUD)

A ____________________

____

C ____________________

____

Situation 2 (medium SUD)

A ____________________

____

C ____________________

____

Situation 3 (high SUD)

A ____________________

____

C ____________________

____

Most believable thought: ____________________

____

____

Situation 1 (low SUD)

A ____________________

____

C ____________________

____

Situation 2 (medium SUD)

A ____________________

____

C ____________________

____

Situation 3 (high SUD)

A ____________________

____

C ____________________

____

Appendix E
Record Sheet

ASSIGNMENT: Do VCI, SP–SR, or other techniques for 20 to 30 minutes each day. Record your results on the chart below.

Date	Technique	Number of Repetitions	SUD Before	SUD After

Appendix F
Perceptual Shift Worksheet

A (situation): ____

____

____

C (emotion): ____

____

____

Bs (thoughts)	True or False	General Counters to Bs	Details of Counters (experiences that prove counters are not true)

Author Index

Subject Index

a b c d e f g h i j
1 2
8